CW00739709

HISTORICAL RECORD

OF

THE TWENTY-SECOND,

OR

THE CHESHIRE REGIMENT OF FOOT.

CONTAINING

AN ACCOUNT OF THE FORMATION OF THE REGIMENT

IN 1689,

AND OF ITS SUBSEQUENT SERVICES

TO 1849.

COMPILED BY

RICHARD CANNON, Esq.,

ADJUTANT-GENERAL'S OFFICE, HORSE GUARDS.

ILLUSTRATED WITH PLATES.

LONDON:

PARKER, FURNIVALL, & PARKER,

30, CHARING-CROSS.

MDCCCXLIX.

GENERAL ORDERS.

HORSE-GUARDS,

1st January, 1836.

His Majesty has been pleased to command that, with the view of doing the fullest justice to Regiments, as well as to Individuals who have distinguished themselves by their Bravery in Action with the Enemy, an Account of the Services of every Regiment in the British Army shall be published under the superintendence and direction of the Adjutant-General; and that this Account shall contain the following particulars, viz.:—

—— The Period and Circumstances of the Original Formation of the Regiment; The Stations at which it has been from time to time employed; The Battles, Sieges, and other Military Operations in which it has been engaged, particularly specifying any Achievement it may have performed, and the Colours, Trophies, &c., it may have captured from the Enemy.

—— The Names of the Officers, and the number of Non-Commissioned Officers and Privates Killed or Wounded by the Enemy, specifying the place and Date of the Action.

a

—— The Names of those Officers who, in consideration of their Gallant Services and Meritorious Conduct in Engagements with the Enemy, have been distinguished with Titles, Medals, or other Marks of His Majesty's gracious favour.

—— The Names of all such Officers, Non-Commissioned Officers, and Privates, as may have specially signalized themselves in Action.

And,

—— The Badges and Devices which the Regiment may have been permitted to bear, and the Causes on account of which such Badges or Devices, or any other Marks of Distinction, have been granted.

By Command of the Right Honorable

GENERAL LORD HILL,

Commanding-in-Chief.

JOHN MACDONALD,
Adjutant-General.

PREFACE.

THE character and credit of the British Army must chiefly depend upon the zeal and ardour by which all who enter into its service are animated, and consequently it is of the highest importance that any measure calculated to excite the spirit of emulation, by which alone great and gallant actions are achieved, should be adopted.

Nothing can more fully tend to the accomplishment of this desirable object than a full display of the noble deeds with which the Military History of our country abounds. To hold forth these bright examples to the imitation of the youthful soldier, and thus to incite him to emulate the meritorious conduct of those who have preceded him in their honorable career, are among the motives that have given rise to the present publication.

The operations of the British Troops are, indeed, announced in the " London Gazette," from whence they are transferred into the public prints: the achievements of our armies are thus made known at the time of their occurrence, and receive the tribute

of praise and admiration to which they are entitled.
On extraordinary occasions, the Houses of Parliament
have been in the habit of conferring on the Commanders, and the Officers and Troops acting under
their orders, expressions of approbation and of thanks
for their skill and bravery; and these testimonials,
confirmed by the high honour of their Sovereign's
approbation, constitute the reward which the soldier
most highly prizes.

It has not, however, until late years, been the practice (which appears to have long prevailed in some of
the Continental armies) for British Regiments to keep
regular records of their services and achievements.
Hence some difficulty has been experienced in obtain-
ing, particularly from the old Regiments, an authentic account of their origin and subsequent services.

This defect will now be remedied, in consequence
of His Majesty having been pleased to command
that every Regiment shall, in future, keep a full and
ample record of its services at home and abroad.

From the materials thus collected, the country
will henceforth derive information as to the difficulties
and privations which chequer the career of those who
embrace the military profession. In Great Britain,
where so large a number of persons are devoted to
the active concerns of agriculture, manufactures,
and commerce, and where these pursuits have, for so

long a period, being undisturbed by the *presence of war*, which few other countries have escaped, comparatively little is known of the vicissitudes of active service and of the casualties of climate, to which, even during peace, the British Troops are exposed in every part of the globe, with little or no interval of repose.

In their tranquil enjoyment of the blessings which the country derives from the industry and the enterprise of the agriculturist and the trader, its happy inhabitants may be supposed not often to reflect on the perilous duties of the soldier and the sailor,—on their sufferings,—and on the sacrifice of valuable life, by which so many national benefits are obtained and preserved.

The conduct of the British Troops, their valour, and endurance, have shone conspicuously under great and trying difficulties; and their character has been established in Continental warfare by the irresistible spirit with which they have effected debarkations in spite of the most formidable opposition, and by the gallantry and steadiness with which they have maintained their advantages against superior numbers.

In the official Reports made by the respective Commanders, ample justice has generally been done to the gallant exertions of the Corps employed; but the details of their services and of acts of individual bravery can only be fully given in the Annals of the various Regiments.

These Records are now preparing for publication, under his Majesty's special authority, by Mr. RICHARD CANNON, Principal Clerk of the Adjutant General's Office; and while the perusal of them cannot fail to be useful and interesting to military men of every rank, it is considered that they will also afford entertainment and information to the general reader, particularly to those who may have served in the Army, or who have relatives in the Service.

There exists in the breasts of most of those who have served, or are serving, in the Army, an *Esprit de Corps*—an attachment to everything belonging to their Regiment; to such persons a narrative of the services of their own Corps cannot fail to prove interesting.   Authentic accounts of the actions of the great, the valiant, the loyal, have always been of paramount interest with a brave and civilized people.   Great Britain has produced a race of heroes who, in moments of danger and terror, have stood "firm as the rocks of their native shore:" and when half the world has been arrayed against them, they have fought the battles of their Country with unshaken fortitude.   It is presumed that a record of achievements in war,—victories so complete and surprising, gained by our countrymen, our brothers, our fellow citizens in arms,—a record which revives the memory of the brave, and brings their gallant deeds before us,—will certainly prove acceptable to the public.

Biographical Memoirs of the Colonels and other distinguished Officers will be introduced in the Records of their respective Regiments, and the Honorary Distinctions which have, from time to time, been conferred upon each Regiment, as testifying the value and importance of its services, will be faithfully set forth.

As a convenient mode of Publication, the Record of each Regiment will be printed in a distinct number, so that when the whole shall be completed, the Parts may be bound up in numerical succession.

INTRODUCTION

TO

THE INFANTRY.

THE natives of Britain have, at all periods, been celebrated for innate courage and unshaken firmness, and the national superiority of the British troops over those of other countries has been evinced in the midst of the most imminent perils. History contains so many proofs of extraordinary acts of bravery, that no doubts can be raised upon the facts which are recorded. It must therefore be admitted, that the distinguishing feature of the British soldier is INTREPIDITY. This quality was evinced by the inhabitants of England when their country was invaded by Julius Cæsar with a Roman army, on which occasion the undaunted Britons rushed into the sea to attack the Roman soldiers as they descended from their ships; and, although their discipline and arms were inferior to those of their adversaries, yet their fierce and dauntless bearing intimidated the flower of the Roman troops, including Cæsar's favourite tenth legion. Their arms consisted of spears, short swords, and other weapons of rude construction. They had chariots, to the axles of which were fastened sharp pieces of iron resembling scythe-blades, and infantry in long chariots resembling waggons, who alighted and fought on foot, and for change of ground, pursuit or retreat, sprang into the chariot and drove off with the speed of cavalry. These inventions were, however, unavailing against Cæsar's legions: in the course of time a military system, with discipline and subordination, was introduced, and British courage, being thus regulated, was exerted to the greatest advantage; a full development of the national character followed, and it shone forth in all its native brilliancy.

The military force of the Anglo-Saxons consisted principally of infantry: Thanes, and other men of property, however, fought on horseback. The infantry were of two classes, heavy and light. The former carried large shields armed with spikes, long broad swords and spears; and the latter were armed with swords or spears only. They had also men armed with clubs, others with battle-axes and javelins.

The feudal troops established by William the Conqueror consisted (as already stated in the Introduction to the Cavalry) almost entirely of horse; but when the warlike barons and knights, with their trains of tenants and vassals, took the field, a proportion of men appeared on foot, and, although these were of inferior degree, they proved stout-hearted Britons of stanch fidelity. When stipendiary troops were employed, infantry always constituted a considerable portion of the military force;

and this *arme* has since acquired, in every quarter of the globe, a celebrity never exceeded by the armies of any nation at any period.

The weapons carried by the infantry, during the several reigns succeeding the Conquest, were bows and arrows, half-pikes, lances, halberds, various kinds of battle-axes, swords, and daggers. Armour was worn on the head and body, and in course of time the practice became general for military men to be so completely cased in steel, that it was almost impossible to slay them.

The introduction of the use of gunpowder in the destructive purposes of war, in the early part of the fourteenth century, produced a change in the arms and equipment of the infantry-soldier. Bows and arrows gave place to various kinds of fire-arms, but British archers continued formidable adversaries; and, owing to the inconvenient construction and imperfect bore of the fire-arms when first introduced, a body of men, well trained in the use of the bow from their youth, was considered a valuable acquisition to every army, even as late as the sixteenth century.

During a great part of the reign of Queen Elizabeth each company of infantry usually consisted of men armed five different ways; in every hundred men forty were "*men-at-arms*," and sixty "*shot*;" the "men-at-arms" were ten halberdiers, or battle-axe men, and thirty pikemen; and the "shot" were twenty archers, twenty musketeers, and twenty harquebusiers, and each man carried, besides his principal weapon, a sword and dagger.

Companies of infantry varied at this period in numbers from 150 to 300 men ; each company had a colour or ensign, and the mode of formation recommended by an English military writer (Sir John Smithe) in 1590 was :—the colour in the centre of the company guarded by the halberdiers; the pikemen in equal proportions, on each flank of the halberdiers: half the musketeers on each flank of the pikes ; half the archers on each flank of the musketeers, and the harquebusiers (whose arms were much lighter than the muskets then in use) in equal proportions on each flank of the company for skirmishing.* It was customary to unite a number of companies into one body, called a REGIMENT, which frequently amounted to three thousand men: but each company continued to carry a colour. Numerous improvements were eventually introduced in the construction of fire-arms, and, it having been found impossible to make armour proof against the muskets then in use (which carried a very heavy ball) without its being too weighty for the soldier, armour was gradually laid aside by the infantry in the seventeenth century : bows and arrows also fell into disuse, and the infantry were reduced to two classes, viz.: *musketeers*, armed with matchlock muskets,

---

* A company of 200 men would appear thus :—

20	20	20	30	20	30	20	20	20
Harquebuses.	Archers.	Muskets.	Pikes.	Halberds.	Pikes.	Muskets.	Archers.	Harquebuses.

The musket carried a ball which weighed $\frac{1}{10}$th of a pound ; and the harquebus a ball which weighed $\frac{1}{5}$th of a pound.

swords, and daggers ; and *pikemen*, armed with pikes from fourteen to eighteen feet long, and swords.

In the early part of the seventeenth century Gustavus Adolphus, King of Sweden, reduced the strength of regiments to 1000 men. He caused the gunpowder, which had heretofore been carried in flasks, or in small wooden bandoliers, each containing a charge, to be made up into cartridges, and carried in pouches; and he formed each regiment into two wings of musketeers, and a centre division of pikemen. He also adopted the practice of forming four regiments into a brigade ; and the number of colours was afterwards reduced to three in each regiment. He formed his columns so compactly that his infantry could resist the charge of the celebrated Polish horsemen and Austrian cuirassiers ; and his armies became the admiration of other nations. His mode of formation was copied by the English, French, and other European states ; but so great was the prejudice in favour of ancient customs, that all his improvements were not adopted until near a century afterwards.

In 1664 King Charles II. raised a corps for sea-service, styled the Admiral's regiment. In 1678 each company of 100 men usually consisted of 30 pikemen, 60 musketeers, and 10 men armed with light firelocks. In this year the King added a company of men armed with hand grenades to each of the old British regiments, which was designated the " grenadier company." Daggers were so contrived as to fit in the muzzles of the muskets, and bayonets similar to those at present in use were adopted about twenty years afterwards.

An Ordnance regiment was raised in 1685, by order of King James II., to guard the artillery, and was designated the Royal Fusiliers (now 7th Foot). This corps, and the companies of grenadiers, did not carry pikes.

King William III. incorporated the Admiral's regiment in the second Foot Guards, and raised two Marine regiments for sea-service. During the war in this reign, each company of infantry (excepting the fusiliers and grenadiers) consisted of 14 pikemen and 46 musketeers; the captains carried pikes; lieutenants, partisans; ensigns, half-pikes; and serjeants, halberds. After the peace in 1697 the Marine regiments were disbanded, but were again formed on the breaking out of the war in 1702.*

During the reign of Queen Anne the pikes were laid aside, and every infantry soldier was armed with a musket, bayonet, and sword; the grenadiers ceased, about the same period, to carry hand grenades; and the regiments were directed to lay aside their third colour: the corps of Royal Artillery was first added to the Army in this reign.

About the year 1745, the men of the battalion companies of infantry ceased to carry swords; during

---

* The 30th, 31st, and 32nd Regiments were formed as Marine corps in 1702, and were employed as such during the wars in the reign of Queen Anne. The Marine corps were embarked in the Fleet under Admiral Sir George Rooke, and were at the taking of Gibraltar, and in its subsequent defence in 1704; they were afterwards employed at the siege of Barcelona in 1705.

the reign of George II. light companies were added to infantry regiments; and in 1764 a Board of General Officers recommended that the grenadiers should lay aside their swords, as that weapon had never been used during the Seven Years' War. Since that period the arms of the infantry soldier have been limited to the musket and bayonet.

The arms and equipment of the British Troops have seldom differed materially, since the Conquest, from those of other European states; and in some respects the arming has, at certain periods, been allowed to be inferior to that of the nations with whom they have had to contend; yet, under this disadvantage, the bravery and superiority of the British infantry have been evinced on very many and most trying occasions, and splendid victories have been gained over very superior numbers.

Great Britain has produced a race of lion-like champions who have dared to confront a host of foes, and have proved themselves valiant with any arms. At *Crecy*, King Edward III., at the head of about 30,000 men, defeated, on the 26th of August, 1346, Philip King of France, whose army is said to have amounted to 100,000 men; here British valour encountered veterans of renown:—the King of Bohemia, the King of Majorca, and many princes and nobles were slain, and the French army was routed and cut to pieces. Ten years afterwards, Edward Prince of Wales, who was designated the Black Prince, defeated, at *Poictiers*, with 14,000 men, a French army of 60,000 horse, besides infantry, and took John I., King of France, and his son

Philip, prisoners. On the 25th of October, 1415, King Henry V., with an army of about 13,000 men, although greatly exhausted by marches, privations, and sickness, defeated, at *Agincourt*, the Constable of France, at the head of the flower of the French nobility and an army said to amount to 60,000 men, and gained a complete victory.

During the seventy years' war between the United Provinces of the Netherlands and the Spanish monarchy, which commenced in 1578 and terminated in 1648, the British infantry in the service of the States-General were celebrated for their unconquerable spirit and firmness;* and in the thirty years' war between the Protestant Princes and the Emperor of Germany, the British Troops in the service of Sweden and other states were celebrated for deeds of heroism.† In the wars of Queen Anne, the fame of the British army under the great MARLBOROUGH was spread throughout the world; and if we glance at the achievements performed within the memory of persons now living, there is abundant proof that the Britons of the present age are not inferior to their ancestors in the qualities

---

* The brave Sir Roger Williams, in his Discourse on War, printed in 1590, observes:—" I persuade myself ten thousand of our nation would beat thirty thousand of theirs (the Spaniards) out of the field, let them be chosen where they list." Yet at this time the Spanish infantry was allowed to be the best disciplined in Europe. For instances of valour displayed by the British Infantry during the Seventy Years' War, see the Historical Record of the Third Foot, or Buffs.

† *Vide* the Historical Record of the First, or Royal Regiment of Foot.

which constitute good soldiers. Witness the deeds of the brave men, of whom there are many now surviving, who fought in Egypt in 1801, under the brave Abercromby, and compelled the French army, which had been vainly styled *Invincible*, to evacuate that country; also the services of the gallant Troops during the arduous campaigns in the Peninsula, under the immortal WELLINGTON; and the determined stand made by the British Army at Waterloo, where Napoleon Bonaparte, who had long been the inveterate enemy of Great Britain, and had sought and planned her destruction by every means he could devise, was compelled to leave his vanquished legions to their fate, and to place himself at the disposal of the British Government. These achievements, with others of recent dates, in the distant climes of India, prove that the same valour and constancy which glowed in the breasts of the heroes of Crecy, Poictiers, Agincourt, Blenheim, and Ramilies, continue to animate the Britons of the nineteenth century.

The British Soldier is distinguished for a robust and muscular frame,—intrepidity which no danger can appal,—unconquerable spirit and resolution,—patience in fatigue and privation, and cheerful obedience to his superiors. These qualities, united with an excellent system of order and discipline to regulate and give a skilful direction to the energies and adventurous spirit of the hero, and a wise selection of officers of superior talent to command, whose presence inspires confidence,—have been the leading causes of the splendid victories gained by the British

b

arms.* The fame of the deeds of the past and present generations in the various battle-fields where the robust sons of Albion have fought and conquered, surrounds the British arms with a halo of glory; these achievements will live in the page of history to the end of time.

The records of the several regiments will be found to contain a detail of facts of an interesting character, connected with the hardships, sufferings, and gallant exploits of British soldiers in the various parts of the world where the calls of their Country and the commands of their Sovereign have required them to proceed in the execution of their duty, whether in

---

* " Under the blessing of Divine Providence, His Majesty ascribes the successes which have attended the exertions of his troops in Egypt to that determined bravery which is inherent in Britons; but His Majesty desires it may be most solemnly and forcibly impressed on the consideration of every part of the army, that it has been a strict observance of order, discipline, and military system, which has given the full energy to the native valour of the troops, and has enabled them proudly to assert the superiority of the national military character, in situations uncommonly arduous, and under circumstances of peculiar difficulty."—*General Orders in* 1801.

In the General Orders issued by Lieut.-General Sir John Hope (afterwards Lord Hopetoun), congratulating the army upon the successful result of the Battle of Corunna, on the 16th of January, 1809, it is stated:—" On no occasion has the undaunted valour of British troops ever been more manifest. At the termination of a severe and harassing march, rendered necessary by the superiority which the enemy had acquired, and which had materially impaired the efficiency of the troops, many disadvantages were to be encountered. These have all been surmounted by the conduct of the troops themselves: and the enemy has been taught, that whatever advantages of position or of numbers he may possess, there is inherent in the British officers and soldiers a bravery that knows not how to yield,—that no circumstances can appal,—and that will ensure victory, when it is to be obtained by the exertion of any human means.

active continental operations, or in maintaining colonial territories in distant and unfavourable climes.

The superiority of the British infantry has been pre-eminently set forth in the wars of six centuries, and admitted by the greatest commanders which Europe has produced. The formations and movements of this *arme*, as at present practised, while they are adapted to every species of warfare, and to all probable situations and circumstances of service, are calculated to show forth the brilliancy of military tactics calculated upon mathematical and scientific principles. Although the movements and evolutions have been copied from the continental armies, yet various improvements have from time to time been introduced, to insure that simplicity and celerity by which the superiority of the national military character is maintained. The rank and influence which Great Britain has attained among the nations of the world, have in a great measure been purchased by the valour of the Army, and to persons who have the welfare of their country at heart, the records of the several regiments cannot fail to prove interesting.

THE TWENTY-SECOND,

OR

THE CHESHIRE REGIMENT OF FOOT.

CONTENTS

OF THE

HISTORICAL RECORD.

SUCCESSION OF COLONELS

OF

THE TWENTY-SECOND,

OR

THE CHESHIRE REGIMENT OF FOOT.

PLATES.

HISTORICAL RECORD

OF

THE TWENTY-SECOND,

OR

THE CHESHIRE REGIMENT OF FOOT.

THE accession of King William III. and Queen Mary, in February, 1689, was welcomed in England with anticipations of security to the civil and religious institutions of the country, and of prosperity in every branch of national industry; but in Ireland the majority of the people adhered to the interests of the Stuart dynasty, and a body of troops was raised in England, for the deliverance of that country from the power of King James, who had landed there with an armament from France. · On this occasion HENRY, DUKE OF NORFOLK, evinced zeal for the principles of the Revolution, and raised a regiment of pikemen and musketeers, to which a company of grenadiers was attached; and the corps raised under the auspices of his Grace now bears the title of the TWENTY-SECOND, or the CHESHIRE REGIMENT OF FOOT.

Having been speedily completed in numbers, equipped, and disciplined, the regiment was encamped near Chester in the early part of August, and soon afterwards embarked for Ireland, with the forces commanded by Marshal

B

1689 Duke Schomberg.   On landing in Ireland, the siege of *Carrickfergus* was commenced, and the garrison of that fortress was forced to surrender in a few days.

From Carrickfergus, the regiment marched with the army to Dundalk, where the troops were encamped on low and wet ground, and suffered much in their health.

While the regiment was encamped at Dundalk, the Duke of Norfolk was succeeded in the colonelcy by Sir Henry Bellasis, who had commanded the Sixth regiment of foot when it was in the Dutch service.

On the 7th of November the regiment commenced its march from Dundalk for Armagh, for winter-quarters.

1690   In the summer of 1690, the regiment had the honour to serve at the battle of the *Boyne,* under the eye of its Sovereign, who commanded the army in Ireland in person ; and on this occasion it took part in forcing the passage of the river, and in gaining a decisive victory over the army of King James on the 1st of July.

Advancing from the field of battle towards Dublin, the regiment was reviewed by King William at Finglass, on the 8th of July, and mustered six hundred and twenty-eight rank and file under arms.   It was afterwards detached, under Lieut.-General Douglas, against Athlone ; but that fortress was found better provided for a siege than had been expected, and the regiment rejoined the army.

The TWENTY-SECOND was one of the corps employed at the siege of *Limerick.*   Many things combined to prevent the capture of that fortress until the following year, and when the siege was raised, the regiment proceeded into winter-quarters, from whence it sent out detachments, which had several rencounters with bands of armed peasantry, called Rapparees.

1691   On the 6th of June, 1691, the regiment joined the army commanded by Lieut.-General De Ghinkel (afterwards 1691 Earl of Athlone) on its march for *Ballymore*, which fortress was speedily forced to surrender.

From Ballymore, the regiment marched to *Athlone*, and had the honour to take part in the siege of that fortress, which was captured by storm on the 1st of July. The grenadier company of the regiment formed part of the storming party, which forded the river Shannon under a heavy fire, and carried the works with great gallantry. The capture of Athlone is one of the many splendid achievements which have exalted the reputation of the British arms, and its reduction proved a presage of additional triumphs.

Astonished and confounded by the capture of Athlone, General St. Ruth retreated, with the French and Irish army under his orders, to a position at *Aghrim*, where he was attacked on the 12th of July. On this occasion, the regiment formed part of the brigade commanded by its Colonel, Brigadier-General Sir Henry Bellasis, and it contributed towards the complete overthrow of the army of King James, which was driven from the field with severe loss, including its commander, General St. Ruth, who was killed by a cannon-ball.

The regiment had one Ensign and two private soldiers killed ; one Major, and twenty-three soldiers wounded.

On the 19th of July the army approached *Galway ;* after sunset six regiments of foot and four squadrons of horse and dragoons passed the river by pontoons, and on the following morning they captured some outworks. On the 21st the garrison surrendered. Brigadier-General Sir Henry Bellasis was nominated Governor of Galway, and he took possession of the town with the TWENTY-SECOND and two other regiments of foot.

The surrender of Galway was followed by the siege

1691 and capitulation of *Limerick*, which city was surrendered
in September, and completed the deliverance of Ireland
from the power of King James.

1692   After the reduction of Ireland, the regiment was employed in garrison and other duties of home-service,

1695 until 1695, when it proceeded to the Netherlands, to
reinforce the army commanded by King William III.,
who was engaged in war for the preservation of the
liberties of Europe against the power of Louis XIV. of
France.   After landing at Ostend, the regiment was
placed in garrison.

1696   Some advantages had been gained over the French
arms; to counteract which, Louis XIV. attempted to
weaken the confederates by forming plans for causing
England to become the theatre of civil war.   With this
view the Duke of Berwick and several other officers in
the French service were sent to England in disguise, to
instigate the adherents of King James to take arms; a
plot was also formed for the assassination of King William,
and a French army marched to the coast to be in readiness to embark for England.   Under these circumstances
the TWENTY-SECOND regiment and a number of other
corps were ordered to return to England, where they
arrived in March, 1696, and the TWENTY-SECOND landed
at Gravesend.   The conspirators for the assassination of
King William were discovered; several persons were
apprehended, the British fleet was sent to blockade the
French ports, and the designs of Louis XIV. were frustrated.

1697   In the following year a treaty of peace was concluded
at Ryswick, and the British Monarch saw his efforts for
the civil and religious liberties of Europe attended with
success.

1698   The TWENTY-SECOND regiment was afterwards sent to

Ireland, where it was stationed during the remainder of the 1700
reign of King William III.

On the 28th of June, 1701, the colonelcy of the regi- 1701
ment was conferred on Brigadier-General William
Selwyn, in succession to Lieut.-General Sir Henry Bellasis, who was removed to the Second foot, then styled
the Queen Dowager's regiment.

King William died in March, 1702, and was succeeded 1702
by Queen Anne, who declared war against France.
Brigadier-General Selwyn was nominated Governor of
Jamaica, and promoted to the rank of Major-General on
the 10th of June, 1702. The TWENTY-SECOND regiment
was ordered to proceed to Jamaica, and several other
corps also embarked for stations in the West Indies : the
British government designing to make a general attack
on the possessions of France and Spain in South America.

Major-General Selwyn died at Jamaica, and was succeeded in the colonelcy of the regiment by the Lieut.-
Colonel, Thomas Handasyd, by commission dated the 20th
of June, 1702.

A considerable body of troops arrived in the West 1703
Indies in 1703 : but they were afterwards recalled to take
part in the war in Europe. The TWENTY-SECOND regiment was left at the island of Jamaica, and during the
reign of Queen Anne the regiment was employed in
protecting Jamaica, and the other British settlements in
the West Indies, which important duty it performed with
reputation.

While employed on this duty, the regiment received 1704
drafts from several other corps, and in 1705 an augment- 1705
ation of two companies was made to its establishment.

Colonel Handasyd was promoted to the rank of Brigadier-
General in December, 1705, and to that of Major-General
in January, 1710. In 1712 he retired from the colonelcy, 1712

1712 resigning his commission in favour of his son, Lieut.-Colonel Roger Handasyd, of the regiment.

1713   In the following year the treaty of Utrecht gave peace
1714 to Europe; and on the 31st of May, 1714, an order was issued for the men of the regiment fit for duty to be formed into two independent companies for service at Jamaica: the officers and staff returning to Europe to recruit.

The two independent companies thus formed from the TWENTY-SECOND were the nucleus of the FORTY-NINTH regiment, which was formed of independent companies at Jamaica in 1743.

1715   The officers and the serjeants not required for the independent companies, having arrived in England, were
1718 actively employed in recruiting in 1715; and in 1718 the regiment proceeded to Ireland.

1719   The regiment was stationed in Ireland during the eight
1726 years from 1719 to 1726, and in the spring of the last-mentioned year, it proceeded to the island of Minorca, which had been captured by the English, in 1708, and was ceded to Great Britain by the treaty of Utrecht in 1713, together with the fortress of Gibraltar.

1727   In the beginning of 1727, the Spaniards besieged *Gibraltar*, and a detachment of the regiment, being sent to reinforce the garrison, had the honor to take part in the successful defence of that important fortress. When the Spaniards raised the siege, the detachment rejoined the regiment at Minorca.

1730   Colonel Handasyd commanded the regiment with reputation until 1730, when he was removed to the Sixteenth foot, and was succeeded by Brigadier-General William Barrell, from the Twenty-eighth regiment.

1734   Brigadier-General Barrell was removed to the Fourth foot in 1734, when King George II. conferred the colonelcy of the TWENTY-SECOND regiment on Colonel

the Honorable James St. Clair, from Major in the First 1734
foot-guards.

On the 27th of June, 1737, Colonel the Honorable 1737
James St. Clair was removed to the First, the Royal
regiment of foot, and his Majesty nominated Major-
General John Moyle, from the Thirty-sixth, to the colonelcy
of the TWENTY-SECOND regiment.

Major-General Moyle died on the 3rd of November, 1738
1738, and the colonelcy was afterwards conferred on
Colonel Thomas Paget, from the Thirty-second regiment.

In 1739 Colonel Paget was promoted to the rank of 1739
brigadier-general. He died on the 28th of May, 1741, 1741
and was succeeded in the colonelcy of the regiment by
Lieut.-Colonel Richard O'Farrell, from the Ninth foot.

The TWENTY-SECOND regiment was employed in the 1748
protection of the island of Minorca, during the whole of
the War of the Austrian Succession, and, peace having
been concluded, it was relieved from that duty in 1749, 1749
and proceeded to Ireland.

In the Royal Warrant for regulating the uniform and 1751
distinctions of the several regiments of the army, dated
the 1st of July, 1751, the facings of the TWENTY-SECOND
regiment were directed to be of *pale buff*. The First, or
King's colour, was the Great Union ; the Second, or
Regimental colour, was of pale buff silk, with the Union in
the upper canton ; in the centre of the colour, the Number
of the Rank of the regiment, in gold Roman characters,
within a wreath of roses and thistles on the same stalk.

The peace of Aix-la-Chapelle was interrupted in 1755 1755
by the aggressions of the French on the British territory in
North America ; and on the 18th of May, 1756, war was 1756
declared against France ; in the same year the TWENTY-
SECOND regiment embarked from Ireland for North
America.

In 1757 the regiment was formed in brigade with the 1757

1757 Forty-third, Forty-eighth, and fourth battalion of the
Sixtieth, under Major-General Lord Charles Hay, with
the view of being employed in the attack of *Louisburg*,
the capital of the French island of *Cape Breton*, situate
in the Gulf of St. Lawrence; but the expedition was
deferred until the following year, and the regiment was
stationed in Nova Scotia during the winter.   Major-
General O'Farrell died in the summer of this year, and the
colonelcy of the regiment was conferred on Brigadier-
General Edward Whitmore, from the lieut.-colonelcy of
the Thirty-sixth regiment.

1758 Embarking from Halifax, in May, 1758, under the
command of Lieut.-Colonel Andrew Lord Rollo, the
regiment proceeded with the expedition commanded by
Lieut.-General (afterwards Lord) Amherst, and a landing
was effected on the island of Cape Breton, on the 8th
of June, when the British troops evinced great gallantry.
The TWENTY-SECOND had Lieutenants Pierce Butler,
John Jermyn, and William Hamilton wounded; also
several private soldiers killed and wounded.*

The siege of *Louisburg*, the capital of the island, was
afterwards commenced; and in carrying on the approaches
the troops underwent great fatigue with cheerful alacrity.
By their perseverance, and the co-operation of the fleet,
the town was taken in July, and two other islands in the
Gulf were surrendered.   The troops received the thanks
of Parliament, and the approbation of the Sovereign, for
their conduct on this occasion.

1759 During the year 1759 the TWENTY-SECOND regiment
was stationed at Louisburg.   Major-General James
Wolfe proceeded up the river St. Lawrence, with a small

---

* Cape Breton had been captured by the British in 1745, but was
restored to the French at the peace of Aix-la-Chapelle in 1748.
It was retaken in 1758 (as above narrated), and was finally ceded to
Great Britain by the treaty of Fontainebleau, in 1763.

armament,* and Quebec was captured; but the nation 1759
sustained the loss of Major-General Wolfe, who was
killed in the battle on the heights of Abraham, in front
of Quebec, on the 13th of September, 1759.

In the spring of 1760 the TWENTY-SECOND and Fortieth 1760
regiments proceeded from Louisburg, under Colonel
Lord Rollo, of the TWENTY-SECOND, up the river St.
Lawrence, to Quebec, from whence they advanced upon
Montreal, with the troops under Brigadier-General the
Honorable James Murray. The French possessions in
Canada were invaded at three points, and the Governor
concentrated his forces at Montreal; but he was unable
to withstand the valour and discipline of British troops,
commanded by officers of talent and experience; he
therefore surrendered Montreal, and with it all Canada,
the French battalions becoming prisoners of war. The
TWENTY-SECOND had thus the honor of taking part in the
conquest of the two fine provinces of Upper and Lower
Canada, which have since continued to form part of the
possessions of the British Crown.

After the conquest of Canada, the TWENTY-SECOND 1761
were removed to Albany, from whence they proceeded to
New York, in April, 1761, and afterwards embarked,
under Lord Rollo, for the West Indies.

The island of *Dominica* had been declared neutral; but
it was found to be so much under the influence of France,
and proved a refuge to so many privateers of that nation,
that the British government resolved to take possession of
it. The TWENTY-SECOND, and other corps under
Lord Rollo, landed on the island on the 6th of June,
under cover of the fire of the men-of-war, and drove

---

* The grenadier company of the TWENTY-SECOND regiment, which
had been incorporated with the " *Louisburg Grenadiers*," formed
part of the armament, and was engaged in the battle on the heights
of Abraham on the 13th of September, 1759.

1761 the enemy from his batteries: the grenadiers of the TWENTY-SECOND regiment distinguished themselves on this occasion. In two days the island was reduced to submission with little loss.

1762   From Dominica the TWENTY-SECOND proceeded to Carlisle Bay, Barbadoes, and joined the troops assembled at that place under the orders of Major-General the Honorable Robert Monckton, for the attack of the French island of *Martinique*.   After several attempts on other parts of the island, a landing was effected in Cas des Navières Bay, on the 16th of January, 1762; the works on the heights of *Morne Tortenson* were captured on the 24th of that month; *Morne Garnier* was carried on the 27th; and the citadel of *Fort Royal*. surrendered on the 4th of February.   These successes were followed by the surrender of the opulent city of St. Pierre, and the submission of the whole island to the British Crown.   The Commander of the expedition stated in his despatch—" I " cannot find words to render that ample justice which is " due to the valor of his Majesty's troops which I have " had the honor to command.   The difficulties they had " to encounter in the attack of an enemy possessed of " every advantage of art and nature were great; and " their perseverance in surmounting these obstacles, " furnishes a noble example of British spirit."

The capture of Martinique was followed by that of *Grenada*, *St. Lucia*, and *St. Vincent;* and the acquisition of these islands gave additional honor to the expedition of which the TWENTY-SECOND regiment formed part.

Additional forces arrived in the West Indies, and the TWENTY-SECOND regiment, mustering six hundred and two rank and file, under the command of Major Loftus, joined the expedition commanded by General the Earl of Albemarle, for the reduction of the wealthy and important Spanish city of the *Havannah*, in the island of Cuba

The TWENTY-SECOND, Fortieth, Seventy-second, and five 1762
companies of the Ninetieth, were formed in brigade under
Brigadier-General Lord Rollo.

Proceeding through the Straits of Bahama, the armament
arrived within six leagues of the Havannah on the 6th
of June. A landing was effected on the following day,
and the *Moro* fort, being the key-position of the extensive
works which covered the town, was besieged. This proved
an undertaking of great difficulty; but every obstacle
was overcome by the spirited efforts of the land and sea
forces, and the fort was captured by storm on the 30th of
July. An extensive series of batteries was prepared, and
opened, on the 11th of August, so well-directed a fire on the
works which protected the town, that the guns of the garrison were soon silenced, and the important city of the Havannah was surrendered to the British arms. Nine Spanish
men-of-war were delivered up; two were found upon the
stocks; and three sunk at the entrance of the harbour.

In March of this year Major-General Whitmore, who
was drowned at sea, was succeeded in the colonelcy by
Major-General the Honorable Thomas Gage, from the
Eightieth regiment, a provincial corps which was raised in
1758, and disbanded after the treaty of Fontainebleau.

At the peace of Fontainebleau the *Havannah* was re- 1763
stored to Spain, in exchange for the province of Florida,
on the continent of America; and in 1763 the TWENTY-
SECOND regiment proceeded to *West Florida.*

The regiment was stationed in Florida during the year 1764
1764, and in 1765 it was relieved from duty in that 1765
province, and embarked for Great Britain.

From 1766 to 1769 the regiment was employed at 1766
various stations in England; during the years 1770, 1770
1771, and 1772, it performed duty in Scotland; and in 1772
1773 it proceeded to Ireland.   1773

1775   While the TWENTY-SECOND were stationed in Ireland the misunderstanding between the English government and the British provinces in North America, on the subject of taxation, was followed by hostilities. The regiment embarked from Ireland for North America in 1775, and joined the troops at Boston under General Gage.

During the night of the 16th of June the Americans commenced fortifying the heights on the peninsula of Charlestown, called. *Bunker's Hill;* and on the following day they were attacked by the flank companies of the British corps, and by a few regiments, and driven from their works. The TWENTY-SECOND lost their commanding officer, Lieut.-Colonel James Abercromby, who died of his wounds. He was succeeded by Major James Campbell.

1776   General Sir William Howe assumed the command of the British troops in North America, on General Gage returning to England in October, 1775; in March, 1776, Boston was vacated, when the TWENTY-SECOND proceeded to Nova Scotia.

From Nova Scotia, the regiment sailed with the expedition to Staten Island, near New York; and, additional troops having arrived from Europe, it was formed in brigade with the Forty-third, Fifty-fourth, and Sixty-third, under Brigadier-General Francis Smith.

A landing was effected on *Long Island* on the 22nd of August; and on the 27th of that month the TWENTY-SECOND were engaged in driving the Americans from their positions at *Flat Bush* to their fortified lines at *Brooklyn.* The flank companies had several men killed and wounded on this occasion; the loss of the battalion companies was limited to two men.

The Americans abandoned their lines at Brooklyn, and passed the river to New York. They were followed by

the British, who gained possession of New York, captured 1776
Fort Washington, and reduced a great part of the
Jerseys.

During the winter the regiment was detached, with
several other corps, under Lieut.-Generals Clinton and
Earl Percy, against *Rhode Island.* The regiment embarked on this service in the beginning of December, and
a landing being effected at daybreak on the 9th of that ·
month, the island was speedily reduced to submission.

During the year 1777 the regiment was stationed in 1777
Rhode Island. On the 10th of July the American
Colonel, Barton, arrived at Rhode Island with a few active
men, surprised Major-General Richard Prescott in his
quarters, and conveyed him from the island a prisoner.

In May, 1778, it was ascertained that Major-General 1778
Sullivan had taken the command of the American troops
at Providence, with the view of making a descent on
Rhode Island ; and on the night of the 24th of May the
battalion companies of the TWENTY-SECOND, the flank
companies of the Fifty-fourth, and a company of Hessians,
embarked under Lieut.-Colonel CAMPBELL of the TWENTY-
SECOND, to attack the enemy's quarters. After landing
three miles below *Warren,* early on the following morning,
a detachment under Captain SEIR of the TWENTY-SECOND
destroyed a battery at Papasquash Point, making a
Captain and six American artillery men prisoners. Another detachment destroyed a number of boats, a galley
of six twelve pounders, and two sloops, in the Kickamuct
River. The party then marched to Warren, destroyed a
park of artillery, a quantity of stores, and a privateer
sloop. Afterwards proceeding to Bristol, a further
quantity of stores was destroyed. The Americans assembled in great numbers, and fired on the British from
a great distance, but did little injury. Lieutenant

1778 HAMILTON of the TWENTY-SECOND, eight British, and four Hessian soldiers were wounded.

On the 30th of May another detachment, under Major Eyre of the Fifty-fourth, made a successful incursion to a creek near Taunton River, and inflicted a severe loss on the Americans.

The King of France having united with the Americans, a French armament arrived off the coast, and formidable preparations were made for the re-capture of Rhode Island. The French fleet, however, sustained some severe losses from a storm, and from the English navy. A numerous American force under Major-General Sullivan landed at Howland's Ferry, on the 9th of August, and commenced the siege of *Newport,* in defence of which place the TWENTY-SECOND were employed. The place being defended with great resolution, and the Americans being disappointed of aid from the French fleet, they raised the siege, and retired on the 29th of August. The TWENTY-SECOND, Forty-third, and flank companies of the Thirty-eighth and Fifty-fourth regiments, marched under Brigadier General Smith, by the east road, to intercept the retreating enemy. A stand was made by the Americans, and some sharp fighting occurred, in which the TWENTY-SECOND, under Lieut.-Colonel Campbell, highly distinguished themselves. The Americans were driven from *Quakers' Hill,* when they fell back to their works at the north end of the island, from which they afterwards withdrew. Major-General Pigot stated in his public despatch,— " To these particulars I am, in justice, obliged to add " Brigadier-General Smith's report, who, amidst the " general tribute due to the good conduct of every in- " dividual under his command, has particularly dis- " tinguished Lieut.-Colonel CAMPBELL and the TWENTY- " SECOND regiment, on whom, by their position, the

" greatest weight of the action fell." . The regiment had 1778 eleven rank and file killed ; Lieutenant Cleghorn, Ensigns Bareland, Proctor, and Adam, two serjeants, and forty-eight rank and file wounded ; one man missing.

The British Commander-in-Chief in North America, 1779 Lieut.-General Sir Henry Clinton, having resolved to vacate Rhode Island, the regiment embarked from thence on the 25th of October, 1779, and proceeded to New York, where it arrived on the 27th of that month.

During the remainder of the American War the regi- 1780 ment was stationed at New York and the posts in advance of that city.

General the Honorable Thomas Gage was removed 1782 to the Seventeenth Light Dragoons in April, 1782, and King George III. conferred the colonelcy of the TWENTY-SECOND regiment on Major-General Charles O'Hara, from captain and lieut.-colonel in the Second foot-guards.

A letter, dated the 31st of August, 1782, conveyed to the regiment His Majesty's pleasure that it should be designated the TWENTY-SECOND, or the CHESHIRE regiment, in order that a connexion between the corps and that county should be cultivated, with the view of promoting the success of the recruiting service.

The American War having terminated, the regiment 1783 returned to Europe in 1783 and was stationed in South Britain.

In 1785, while the regiment was stationed at Windsor, 1785 under the command of Lieut.-Colonel Crosbie, and furnished the usual guard at the Castle, where his Majesty resided, an " ORDER OF MERIT " was instituted in the corps, with the view of promoting good order and discipline,— the field-officers, captains, and adjutant for the time being, to be members of the order. The order consisted

1785 of THREE CLASSES: the first wore a silver medal gilt, suspended to a blue riband two inches broad, and worn round the neck; the second a silver medal, and the third a bronze medal, similarly worn. The candidates for the third class must have served seven years with an unblemished character; for the second, fourteen; and for the first, twenty-one years. On the 1st of July, the KING was graciously pleased to accept from Lieut.-Colonel Crosbie a medal of the first class of the regimental ORDER OF MERIT: and on the 3rd of that month, the regiment being then encamped in Windsor Forest, assembled on parade, with the non-commissioned officers and soldiers selected to receive medals in front, the rules of the order were read; the corps presented arms, the band played "God save the King;" the members of the order took off their hats, and the commanding officer invested each member with his medal; the drums beating a point of war during the whole time.

1787   In 1787 the regiment proceeded to Guernsey and Jersey, where its establishment was augmented; and it was ordered to be held in readiness for foreign service, in consequence of some revolutionary proceedings in Holland. In October the regiment proceeded to Portsmouth, and its establishment was soon afterwards reduced. Previous to leaving Guernsey, it received the thanks of the Lieut.-Governor for its excellent conduct.

1788   On quitting Portsmouth in 1788 for Chatham, the regiment received a very flattering mark of the high estimation in which its conduct was held by the inhabitants.

1790   The regiment left Chatham and Dover in the spring of 1790, and proceeding to Ireland landed at Cork on the 5th of April.

1791   Major-General Charles O'Hara was removed to the Seventy-fourth Highlanders in April, 1791, and was succeeded in the colonelcy of the TWENTY-SECOND 1791 by Major-General David Dundas, Adjutant-General of the Army in Ireland   .

In 1792, a slight alteration was made in the uniform, 1792 and the establishment was augmented.

Meanwhile a revolution had taken place in France, 1793 and the violent conduct of the republican government in that country occasioned a war between Great Britain and France, which commenced in 1793.   In September of that year the flank companies of the TWENTY-SECOND regiment embarked for the West Indies, for the purpose of taking part in the capture of the French West India islands.   They were followed by the battalion companies in December.

The flank companies joined the armament under General 1794 Sir Charles (afterwards Earl) Grey, who effected a landing at three different points on the island of *Martinique*, in February, 1794, and accomplished in a short period the conquest of that valuable colony.

The grenadier brigade under His Royal Highness Prince Edward, afterwards the Duke of Kent, and the light infantry under Major-General Dundas, were engaged in the conquest of *St. Lucia* in the beginning of April.

After the conquest of St. Lucia, an attack was made on *Guadaloupe*, and that valuable island was speedily rescued from the power of the republican government of France.

The regiment proceeded to the island of Martinique, where it was joined by the flank companies.

Two hundred men, commanded by Lieut.-Colonel Lysaght, proceeded to the island of *St Domingo*, and formed part of the garrison of Cape St. Nicholas Mole: and five companies joined the garrison of *Busy-town*, which place was besieged by the enemy.

In April, the TWENTY-SECOND, Twenty-third, and

C

1794 Forty-first regiments, with some other troops, embarked under the command of Brigadier-General John Whyte, for the attack of *Port-au-Prince*, the capital of the French possessions in the island of *St. Domingo*. A landing was effected on the 31st of May; some severe fighting occurred, in which the TWENTY-SECOND distinguished themselves: *Fort Bizzotton* was captured, and the enemy was forced to abandon *Port-au-Prince*, which was taken possession of by the British troops. The regiment had Captain Wallace killed on this occasion, also several private soldiers killed and wounded. Unfortunately a malignant fever broke out in the town, and the British lost forty officers and six hundred soldiers by disease within two months after the capture of the place.

A detachment of the regiment formed part of the garrison of *Fort Bizzotton*, which was attacked by two thousand of the enemy on the 5th of December. The British defended their post with great gallantry, and repulsed the assailants. Lieutenant Hamilton of the TWENTY-SECOND distinguished himself.

Another portion of the regiment was stationed at Jeremie, and a detachment at Irois.

1795 Having sustained severe loss from the climate of St. Domingo, the regiment was relieved from duty at that island, and returned to England in 1795.

Lieut.-General Dundas was removed to the Seventh Light Dragoons, and the colonelcy of the TWENTY-SECOND was conferred on Major-General William Crosbie, from the Eighty-ninth regiment.

1798 The regiment was stationed in England recruiting its ranks until December, 1798, when it proceeded to Guernsey.

Major-General Crosbie died this year, and was succeeded by Major-General John Graves Simcoe, from the Eighty-first regiment.

In November, 1799, the regiment was withdrawn from 1799
Guernsey, and landed at Portsmouth on the 15th of that
month.

On its return from the West Indies, the regiment
enlisted a number of boys, or youths; and in 1798 it
received drafts of boys, or lads, from other corps; it was
designated a boy regiment, and sent to the Cape of Good
Hope, where the youths, it was conjectured, would be
gradually accustomed to a warm climate, and become
better adapted for service in the East Indies, than recruits
sent direct from Europe to India.

In January and February, 1800, the regiment em- 1800
barked for the Cape of Good Hope, where it arrived in
May and June following. The companies on board of
one transport, the Surat Castle, suffered severely in consequence of their crowded state: the crew was composed
of Lascars, among whom much disease prevailed; the
infection was communicated to the soldiers, and the men
of the TWENTY-SECOND suffered in their health; sixty
soldiers were sent on shore, to a general hospital, before
the ship left England. The survivors arrived at the Cape
in a sickly state; they had been obliged to aid in working
the vessel during the voyage, and the masts and rigging
had been damaged during a gale of wind.

The head-quarters were established at Muisenberg,
and afterwards encamped at Wynberg, a tongue of land
projecting from the east side of Table Mountain. The
sick men received every attention which could be procured
by Major-General Francis Dundas, commanding at the
Cape, and as they recovered they joined the head-quarters,
which were removed to Simon's-town in January, 1801, 1801
and again encamped at Wynberg in March. In May
the regiment marched into Cape Town, and in September
joined the camp at Rondebosch.

1801   The lads having become much improved in size and strength, the light infantry company joined the flank battalion ; and the grenadiers were detached to the interior, and stationed at Graaff Reinett.

1802   Leaving the camp in January, 1802, the regiment was removed to Muisenberg, Simon's-town, and Graaff Reinett.

The period having arrived for the regiment to proceed to India, it was joined by a number of volunteers from corps serving at the Cape of Good Hope, and embarked from thence in September, October, and November, when it mustered thirty-one officers, and one thousand and fifty-five non-commissioned officers and soldiers fit for duty.

1803   In February, 1803, the last division of the regiment landed at Fort William, Calcutta, where the other companies had previously arrived.

At this period two powerful chieftains, Dowlat Rao Scindia and Jeswunt Rao Holkar, had usurped the powers of the Peishwa, and were desolating the Mahratta states with war ; and these two chiefs, with the Rajah of Berar, formed a confederacy against the British and their allies. Under these circumstances the flank companies of the regiment embarked from Fort William, and joined the field force, under Lieut.-Colonel Harcourt, assembled for the attack of the province of Cuttack. On entering that province, the troops had to overcome numerous difficulties from the nature of the country, the season of the year, and the resistance of the enemy, which they surmounted with great gallantry.

On the 4th of October, the flank companies of the TWENTY-SECOND regiment highly distinguished themselves at the capture of the fort of *Barrabatta* by storm, when they led the assault, and took several of the enemy's colours. They had one man killed ; Captain Harlston and eight

soldiers wounded. The colours captured by the TWENTY- 1803
SECOND, with some others taken by the Ninth and Nineteenth Native Infantry, were publicly displayed at
Calcutta, and afterwards lodged at Fort William, with
an inscription of the names of the corps by which taken.

The flank companies of the regiment remained in the 1804
field, and the splendid successes of the British arms appeared likely to bring about a speedy termination of the
war ; but hostilities were protracted by the defection of the
Rajah of Bhurtpore. The flank companies of the TWENTY-
SECOND joined the army under Lord Lake : they had two
men killed and three wounded at the capture of *Deeg*, in
December, and were engaged in the attempt to bring the
refractory Rajah Sing to submission by the siege of the
strong fortress of Bhurtpore.

In the meantime, the regiment had commenced its 1805
march from Fort William, for the Upper provinces, and
in January, 1805, it halted and encamped at Benares ;
but resumed its march in February, and proceeded to
Cawnpore.

The siege of *Bhurtpore* was carried on, and the flank
companies were engaged in the unsuccessful attempt to
capture that place by storm on the 9th of January, when
they had eleven men killed and twenty-four wounded.
They were also engaged in the desperate attempt to
capture the place by storm, on the 21st of January, when
they had Captain Menzies and four men killed ; Captains
Lindsay and McNight, Lieutenants Mansergh, Sweetman,
and Caswell, and thirty-one non-commissioned officers and
soldiers, wounded. At the third unsuccessful attack, on
the 21st of February, they had two serjeants and three
soldiers killed ; three serjeants and four soldiers wounded.

Serjeant John Ship, of the regiment, led the forlorn
hope on each occasion, and his gallant conduct was

1805 rewarded with the commission of ensign in the Sixty-fifth regiment.

Rajah Sing submitted, and concluded a treaty of peace with the British: the army withdrew from Bhurtpore, and the surviving officers and soldiers of the flank companies joined the regiment at Cawnpore, in June.

Holkar continued his resistance to the British authority, and Scindia evinced a disposition to renew hostilities. These events occasioned the regiment to quit Cawnpore, in October, to pursue the army of Holkar, who was driven from place to place, until the British troops arrived at the banks of the Hyphasis, or Sutlej, where he submitted, and a treaty of peace was concluded in December. Scindia also concluded a second treaty, and the British power and influence in India were thus augmented and consolidated.

1806   From the banks of the Sutlej, the regiment marched to Delhi, where it arrived in February, 1806, and in March it was removed to Muttra, where it received the thanks of General Lord Lake, and of the Governor-General in Council, for its conduct during the war.

On the 30th of October, General Simcoe, who died in 1806, was succeeded in the colonelcy of the regiment by Lieut.-General Sir James Henry Craig, from the Eighty-sixth foot.

1807   Leaving Muttra in July, 1807, the regiment proceeded to Berhampore, where it arrived on the 7th of August.

1809   Major-General the Honorable Edward Finch was appointed colonel of the regiment on the 18th of September, 1809, from the Fifty-fourth foot, in succession to Sir James Henry Craig, K.B., removed to the Seventy-eighth Highlanders.

1810   The regiment remained at Berhampore until August, 1810, when it embarked in boats, and proceeded to Fort William, in order to form part of the expedition against

the *Mauritius*, under Major-General the Honorable J. 1810
Abercromby. A landing was effected in the bay of
Mapou, on the 29th of November, without opposition,
and on the following day the troops advanced towards the
capital ; being exposed to severe heat, and unable to
procure water, the soldiers became exhausted, and arriving
at the powder-mills, five miles from Port Louis, they halted
near the stream. Resuming the march on the 1st of
December, the troops were opposed by the enemy in
force, and some sharp fighting occurred, in which the
TWENTY-SECOND took part and had several men wounded.
The French were driven from their ground, and they
fell back upon Port Louis; the British took post in front
of the position occupied by the French. Being unable to
withstand the valour and discipline of the invading army,
the governor, General de Caen, surrendered the island to
the British arms.

After the capture of the Mauritius, the regiment was 1811
stationed a short time at that island, and in January it
sent a detachment of five officers and seventy men to Tama-
tave, in the Island of Madagascar. In March and April
the regiment was removed to the island of Bourbon, where
it was joined by the survivors of the detachment from
Madagascar, reduced in number, by disease, to two officers
and twenty-five men : they had been made prisoners by
the enemy, and re-captured by the British ships of war.

In July, 1812, the regiment returned to the Mauritius ; 1812
but again proceeded to Bourbon, in August, and was
removed to the Mauritius a second time in May, 1813. 1813

A number of men having volunteered from the militia 1814
to the TWENTY-SECOND regiment, His Royal Highness
the Prince Regent was pleased to approve of a *second
battalion* being formed, and it was placed on the establishment of the army on the 10th of February, 1814.
The war in Europe being terminated soon afterwards, by

1815 the abdication of Napoleon Bonaparte, and the restoration
of the Bourbon dynasty to the throne of France, the second
battalion was disbanded at Chester, on the 24th of October,
transferring the men fit for duty to the first battalion,
which they joined at the Mauritius, in April, 1815, in so
good a state, as' to be specially noticed in general orders,
and Captain Thomas Poole, commanding the party,
received the thanks of the governor.

On the 1st of June, 1815, the rifle company of the first
battalion of the Twelfth regiment, together with the first
battalion of the Eighty-seventh regiment, and the flank
companies of the TWENTY-SECOND regiment, were formed
into a field brigade, and on the 16th of June embarked
from the Mauritius to join the army in Bengal.   The
troops arrived at Bengal on the 2nd and 3rd of August ;
re-embarked on the 23rd of September, and landed at
the Mauritius on the 14th of November, 1815.   The
light company of the TWENTY-SECOND regiment, while
on passage to Bengal, was wrecked in the Straits between
Ceylon and the opposite continent.   The conduct of the
flank companies, while in India, was highly commended
in general orders issued before they embarked from Fort
William,—on their return to the Mauritius.

While the flank companies were thus employed, the remainder of the TWENTY-SECOND regiment was placed
under canvas at Pamplemousse, seven miles from Port
Louis, as it was suffering severely from a prevailing disease at the Mauritius.   There being but a small force
left on the island, and this reduced in numbers and efficiency
by disease, a meditated insurrection had nearly attained
an outbreak, but for timely information.

1819   The regiment occupied various stations at the Mauritius,
under the command of Colonel Dalrymple, until July,
1819, when it embarked for England.   Previous to quitting

the island it was inspected by Major-General Ralph 1819
Darling, who expressed, in general orders, his admiration
of its appearance, and of its excellent conduct while
serving under his command.

Though the TWENTY-SECOND had participated in the
capture of the Mauritius, the French inhabitants of the
island presented a large and handsome gold snuff-box to
the regiment on its embarkation for England, bearing
this inscription, " *Aux Officiers du 22 Régiment de S. M.
—Souvenir des Habitans de l'île Maurice; 1819 ;*" thus
testifying their good feeling, and appreciation of the or-
derly and soldierlike conduct of the corps during its
service of nine years in the colony.

After landing at Gosport, in November and December,
the regiment marched to Northampton, under the orders
of Colonel Sir Hugh Gough, K.C.B.

In the Autumn of 1821 the regiment marched to 1821
Liverpool, where it embarked on the 9th of October, for
Ireland. Having landed at Dublin on the 10th of October,
the regiment marched to Buttevant, with detachments at
Mallow, Bantyre, Charleville, Newmarket, and Bally-
clough.

Some changes of quarters afterwards took place in
consequence of the riotous and violent proceedings of the
misguided peasantry at this part of the country, and the
disposition evinced to violate the law.

On the evening of the 25th of January, 1822, three
thousand men assembled with such arms as they could
procure, for an attack on Newmarket ; and they were
repulsed, with severe loss, by thirty men of the regiment,
under Captain Thomas Keappock and Lieutenant Samuel
Green, who received the expression of the approbation of
His Royal Highness the Duke of York, the Commander-
in-chief, and were presented with a silver cup, by the

1822 noblemen, gentlemen, and inhabitants of the town and vicinity of Newmarket,—" In testimony of the high sense " entertained of their gallant conduct in attacking and " defeating an armed body of three thousand insurgents, " with thirty men."

A reinforcement was sent to Newmarket, and the regiment performed many marches, and much extra duty, in consequence of the disturbed state of the country.

The head-quarters of the regiment were stationed at 1823 Buttevant during the year 1823, and the first nine months 1824 of 1824 ; and the state of the regiment was repeatedly commended in orders by the General Officers who made the half-yearly inspections.

In October, 1824, the regiment marched to Dublin ; it was subsequently stationed in Galway, and in the summer 1826 of 1826 it was divided into six service and four depôt companies, in order that the former might proceed on foreign service.

The service companies embarked from Cork in November and December, in three divisions, commanded by Lieut.-Colonel P. C. Taylor, Major James Steuart, and Captain Thomas Poole, and the last division arrived at the island of Jamaica in February, 1827.

1827   The service companies suffered severely from the effects of the climate of Jamaica ; in September and October, 1827, they lost three officers, seventeen serjeants, and one hundred and twenty men, from fever ; the total loss during the first year was Lieut.-Colonel P. C. Taylor, Major James Steuart, Captain William Norton, Lieutenant Edward Gordon, Ensign E. T. Evans, Paymaster R. Barlow, Adjutant William Potenger, and one hundred and seventy-two non-commissioned officers and soldiers.

1828   In the following year the losses were much less nume-
1829 rous ; and in April, 1829, Lieut.-Colonel· C. G. Falconar

arrived and assumed the command.   In June of the same 1829
year, the regiment received the thanks of the civil authorities for the prompt assistance rendered in extinguishing
an alarming fire in the vicinity of Spanish Town.

On the 7th of June, 1830, the depôt companies em- 1830
barked from Cork for South Britain, where they were
stationed until the summer of 1836, when they embarked
from Liverpool for Ireland, and landed at Dublin.

The regiment was employed in suppressing a formi- 1831
dable insurrection among the slaves in Jamaica in the
winter of 1831-2; the two flank companies were
encamped on the scene of the insurrection in the following winter, and when the regiment left Falmouth, in
Jamaica, in the latter part of the year 1833, the thanks
of the custos and magistrates were awarded to the corps
for its good conduct.*

The service companies performed duty at the island of 1837
Jamaica until the beginning of 1837, when they commenced embarking for Europe, and landed at Cork in
March and April; they were afterwards joined by the
depôt companies.

The regiment remained in Ireland during the years 1838
1838 and 1839; and embarking from Dublin on the 19th 1839
of December, 1840, landed at Liverpool on the 21st of 1840
that month.

The TWENTY-SECOND regiment, having been selected

* When the Marquis of Normanby (then Earl of Mulgrave) presented the regiment with New Colours at Jamaica, he remarked, in
reference to the conduct of the regiment,—" I had myself the
" means of knowing upon the many times I have been at Falmouth,
" whilst your head-quarters were there, that the regiment was univer-
" sally popular, and their departure generally regretted.   During the
" few pleasant days I passed at Shuttlewood, in the camp of which the
" flank companies of the TWENTY-SECOND regiment formed a part, I
" remember upon remarking to the Major-General there commanding,
" the perfect good conduct of all there, he said, ' Yes, I never knew
" better men.' "

1841   to proceed to India, embarked from Gravesend in January, 1841, and landed at Bombay in May following.   It afterwards proceeded to Poonah, where an encampment was formed, and the regiment was stationed there during the remainder of the year.

1842   In the following year the regiment quitted the camp at Poonah by divisions, and proceeding to the country of Scinde, was encamped some time near Kurrachee.   The regiment was encamped in two separate divisions at Kurrachee, as cholera had broken out violently in its ranks, from which it suffered severely, and during its prevalence a field-officer's detachment, under Major Poole, consisting of two companies, was ordered to proceed by the Indus, in the month of April, 1842, to Sukkur, in Upper Scinde, previously to the withdrawal of the British force from Beloochistan.

The navigation of the Indus had been acquired by the British in 1839, and application was made to the Ameers, who governed the country, for a portion of land on the banks of the river.   This they agreed to give; but at the same time meditated the destruction of the British power in the country by treachery.   The TWENTY-SECOND quitted the camp at Kurrachee in November, and proceeded up the country.

1843   The regiment formed part of the force assembled under Major-General Sir Charles Napier, and was employed in the destruction of the fort of *Emaum Ghur*, in the desert, on the 14th and 15th of January, 1843.

Major-General W. F. P. Napier, in his work entitled " *The Conquest of Scinde*," has given, with his characteristic eloquence, the following spirited description of the march to *Emaum Ghur*, a march which His Grace the Duke of Wellington described in the House of Lords, " *as one of the most curious military feats he had ever known to*

be performed, or had ever perused an account of in his life. 1843
Sir Charles Napier (added His Grace) *moved his troops
through the desert against hostile forces ; he had his guns
transported under circumstances of extreme difficulty, and
in a manner the most extraordinary ; and he cut off a retreat
of the enemy which rendered it impossible for them ever to
regain their positions.*"

 " It was a wild and singular country, the wilderness
" through which they (the Anglo-Indian troops) were
" passing.   The sand-hills stretched north and south for
" hundreds of miles in parallel ridges, rounded at top, and
" most symmetrically plaited, like the ripple on the sea-
" shore after a placid tide.   Varying in their heights,
" their breadth and steepness, they presented one uniform
" surface, but while some were only a mile broad, others
" were more than ten miles across ; some were of gentle
" slopes and low, others lofty, and so steep that the
" howitzers could only be dragged up by men.   The
" sand was mingled with shells, and ran in great streams
" resembling numerous rivers, skirted on each side by
" parallel streaks of soil, which nourished jungle, yet
" thinly and scattered.   The tracks of the hyena and
" wild boar, and the prints of small deer's footsteps, were
" sometimes seen at first, but they soon disappeared, and
" then the solitude of the waste was unbroken.

 " For eight days these intrepid soldiers traversed this
" gloomy region, living from hand to mouth, uncertain
" each morning if water could be found in the evening ;
" and many times it was not found.   They were not even
" sure of their right course ; yet with fiery valour and
" untiring strength, they continued their dreary dangerous
" way.   The camels found very little food, and got weak,
" but the stout infantry helped to drag the heavy howit-
" zers up the sandy steeps ; and all the troops, despising

1843 " the danger of an attack from the Beloochees, worked
" with a power and will that overcame every obstacle.
" On the eighth day they reached *Emaum Ghur*, eager
" to strike and storm, and then was seen how truly laid
" down is Napoleon's great maxim, that moral force is in
" war to physical force, as four to one.   Mahomed Khan,
" with a strong fortress well provided, and having a gar-
" rison six times as numerous as the band coming to
" assail him, had fled with his treasure two days before;
" taking a southerly direction, he regained the Indus by
" tracks with which his people were well acquainted,
" leaving all his stores of grain and powder behind."

As Emaum Ghur could only serve as a stronghold in
which the Beloochees might be able to resist British
supremacy, Major-General Sir Charles Napier determined
upon destroying the fortress.   It was a place of great
strength, and was constructed of unburnt bricks, into
which the shot easily penetrates, but brings nothing
down, so that recourse was had to mining.   The place
was full of gunpowder and grain, and the former was
employed in blowing up the fortress, which was effected
on the 15th of January.

After this difficult and harassing service, the troops
returned triumphant on the 23rd of January, to Peer-
Abu-Bekr, where Major-General Sir Charles Napier re-
united his whole army.   It is to be observed that the
march was performed without the loss of a man, or without even a sick soldier, and the Ameers' troops were dis-
persed, and their plan of campaign frustrated.

A treaty of peace was signed by the Ameers on the
14th of February: directions were sent to the British
political resident, Major Outram, by the Ameers, to
quit *Hyderabad*, the capital, and before this was complied
with, *eight thousand* Beloochees, commanded by several

Ameers in person, attempted to force an entrance into 1843 the enclosure of the British residency. The light company of the TWENTY-SECOND regiment, mustering *one hundred* men, under Captain T. S. Conway, Lieutenant F. P. Harding, and Ensign R. Pennefather, was the only force at the residency, the enclosure of which was surrounded by a wall from four to five feet high. The gallant officers and soldiers of this company kept the eight thousand Scindian troops, with six pieces of artillery, at bay nearly four hours; and when their ammunition was nearly expended, they retreated to the river, with Major Outram, and embarking on board of two steam-vessels, joined the troops under Major-General Sir Charles Napier, at Hala. The light company had two men killed and four wounded on this occasion.

The Ameers having thus commenced hostilities, assembled a numerous force to destroy the few British troops in the country. Major-General Sir Charles Napier, trusting to the valour of the troops under his orders, advanced to meet the enemy. On the 17th of February, *twenty-two thousand* Scindian troops were discovered in position behind the bank of a river at *Meeanee.* The British, mustering *two thousand eight hundred* men, advanced in *echelon* of regiments to attack their numerous opponents, and the TWENTY-SECOND, commanded by Lieut.-Colonel J. L. Pennefather, had the honor to lead the attack. A numerous body of Beloochees discharged their matchlocks and pistols at the TWENTY-SECOND, and then rushed forward sword in hand to close upon the British line; but these bold and skilful swordsmen went down under the superior power of the musket and bayonet.

After a severe contest the Scindian army was defeated, and, on the day following the victory, six of the Ameers delivered their swords to the British General upon the

1843 field of battle. The Beloochees lost five thousand men, and all their guns, ammunition, and treasure were taken, together with their camp and standards. On the 20th of February, the British colours waved in triumph over the fortress of *Hyderabad*.

In Major-General Napier's admirable work on " *The Conquest of Scinde*," is given the following spirited and picturesque description of the battle of MEEANEE:—

" The Ameers' right was found to be strengthened and
" covered by the village of Kattree, which was filled with
" men ; that flank offered no weak point. But in the
" Shikargah on their left the General instantly detected
" a flaw. It has been before said this Shikargah was
" covered by a wall, having only one opening, not very
" wide, through which it was evident the Beloochees
" meant to pour out on the flank and rear of the advanc-
" ing British line. The General rode near this wall,
" and found it was nine or ten feet high ; he rode nearer,
" and marked it had no loop-holes for the enemy to
" shoot through ; he rode into the opening under a play
" of matchlocks, and, looking behind the wall, saw there
" was no scaffolding to enable the Beloochees to fire over
" the top. Then the inspiration of genius came to the
" aid of heroism. Taking a company of the TWENTY-
" SECOND, he thrust them at once into the opening, telling
" their brave Captain, Tew, that he was to block up that
" entrance ; to die there, if it must be,—never to give way!
" And well did the gallant fellow obey his orders: he
" died there, but the opening was defended. The great
" disparity of numbers was thus abated, and the action
" of six thousand men paralysed by the more skilful
" action of only eighty! It was, on a smaller scale as to
" numbers, a stroke of generalship like that which won
" Blenheim for the Duke of Marlborough.

" Now the advancing troops, in echelon of regi- 1843
" ments, approached the enemy's front. The British
" right passed securely under the wall of the Shikargah,
" cheered and elated as they moved by the rattling
" sound of Tew's musketry. * * * * Meanwhile the
" dead level of the plain was swept by the Beloochee
" cannon and matchlocks, which were answered from
" time to time by Lloyd's batteries, yet not frequently, for
" rapidly and eagerly did the troops press forward to
" close with their unseen foes. When the TWENTY-
" SECOND had got within a hundred yards of the high
" sloping bank of the Fulaillee, they threw their fire at
" the top of the bank, where the heads of the Beloochees
" could be just seen, bending with fiery glances over
" the levelled matchlocks, and the voice of the General,
" shrill and clear, was heard along the line, commanding
" the charge.

" Then rose the British shout; the English guns were
" run forward into position, the infantry closed upon the
" Fulaillee with a run, and rushed up the sloping bank.
" The Beloochees, having their matchlocks laid ready in
" rest along the summit, waited until the assailants were
" within fifteen yards ere their volley was delivered; the
" rapid pace of the British, and the steepness of the slope
" on the inside, deceived their aim, and the execution
" was not great; the next moment the TWENTY-SECOND
" were on the top of the bank, thinking to bear down all
" before them, but they staggered back in amazement
" at the forest of swords waving in their front! Thick
" as standing corn, and gorgeous as a field of flowers,
" stood the Beloochees in their many-coloured garments
" and turbans; they filled the broad deep bed of the
" Fulaillee, they clustered on both banks, and covered
" the plain beyond. Guarding their heads with their

D

1843 " large dark shields, they shook their sharp swords,
" beaming in the sun, their shouts rolled like a peal of
" thunder, as with frantic gestures they rushed forwards,
" and full against the front of the TWENTY-SECOND
" dashed with demoniac strength and ferocity. But with
" shouts as loud, and shrieks as wild and fierce as theirs,
" and hearts as big, and arms as strong, the Irish soldiers
" met them with that queen of weapons the musket, and
" sent their foremost masses rolling back in blood."

The following extracts from the despatch of Major-
General Sir Charles Napier testify the part borne by the
TWENTY-SECOND in the victory of MEEANEE :—

" Lieutenant - Colonel Pennefather was severely
" wounded as with the high courage of a soldier he
" led his regiment (TWENTY-SECOND) up the desperate
" bank of the Fulaillee.   Major Wyllie, Captains
" Tucker and Conway, Lieutenants Harding and
" Phayre, were all wounded, while gloriously animating
" their men to sustain the shock of numbers."

" Captains Meade, Tew, and Cookson, with Lieutenant
" Wood, all fell honorably, urging on the assault with
" unmitigated valour.

" Major Poole, of the TWENTY-SECOND, and Captain
" Jackson of the Twenty-fifth native infantry, who suc-
" ceeded to the command of those regiments, proved
" themselves worthy of their dangerous posts.

" The   Acting   Assistant   Quartermaster-General,
" Lieutenant McMurdo, of the TWENTY-SECOND regi-
" ment, had his horse killed, and, while on foot leading
" some soldiers in a deperate dash down the enemy's
" side of the bank, he cut down a Chieftain. He has
" greatly assisted me by his activity and zeal during the
" whole of our operations.

" Innumerable are the individual acts of intrepidity

" which took place between our soldiers and their 1843
" opponents, too numerous for detail in this despatch, yet
" well meriting a record."

In the NOTIFICATION of the Right Honorable Lord
Ellenborough, the Governor-General of India, it was
directed,

" That the unserviceable guns, taken at Hyderabad,
" shall be sent to Bombay, and there cast into a triumphal
" column, whereon shall be inscribed in the English, and
" two native languages, the names of Major-General
" Sir Charles Napier, K.C.B., and of the several officers
" mentioned by His Excellency in his despatch, and
" likewise the names of the several officers, non-com-
" missioned officers, and privates mentioned in the reports,
" that thus the names may be for ever recorded of those
" who, at MEEANEE, obtained for themselves that glory in
" the field, which is the reward dearest to a true soldier."

Major Poole, commanding the TWENTY-SECOND regiment, in consequence of Lieutenant-Colonel Pennefather
having been severely wounded, stated in his report,
respecting the soldiers of the regiment under his command, who had distinguished themselves in the battle of
Meeanee, " that the officers generally assert that they
" feel difficulty in making selections, where the conduct
" of every man of their companies was so satisfactory.
" In so general a field of action and persevering exertion,
" I equally feel at a loss where to draw a distinction ;
" but it may be proper to mention the names of Private
" James O'Neill, of the light company, who took a
" standard whilst we were actively engaged with the
" enemy, and drummer Martin Delaney, who shot,
" bayoneted, and captured the arms of Meer Whullee
" Mahomed Khan, who was mounted, and directing the
" enemy in the hottest part of the engagement."

1843   The loss of the TWENTY-SECOND regiment at the battle
of Meeanee was, Captain J. McLeod Tew,* one serjeant,
and twenty-two rank and file killed ; Lieut.-Colonel J. L.
Pennefather, Captain T. S. Conway, Lieutenants W. M.
G. McMurdo and F. P. Harding, Ensigns R. Pennefather and H. Bowden, one serjeant, one corporal, and
fifty privates wounded.

The whole of the Ameers did not submit, and the Chiefs
who continued to resist assembled an army, which was
commanded by Meer Shere Mahomed. The British advanced from *Hyderabad* at daybreak on the morning of
the 24th of March, and about half-past eight o'clock
twenty thousand Scindian troops were discovered in order
of battle behind a nullah. Arrangements were immedi-
ately made for commencing the action, and the TWENTY-
SECOND regiment led the attack in gallant style. Major
John Poole commanded the brigade, and Captain F. D.
George the regiment, and, stimulated by the heroic
example of these officers, the TWENTY-SECOND advanced
steadily against the enemy's left, exposed to a heavy fire
of matchlocks, without returning a shot, until they arrived
within forty paces of the entrenchment, when they stormed
the position occupied by the Beloochees with that determined bravery which has ever distinguished British
soldiers. Lieutenant Henry J. Coote first mounted the
rampart, seized one of the enemy's standards, and was
severely wounded while in the act of waving it, and cheer-
ing on his men ; Lieutenant C. T. Powell seized another
standard ; and the soldiers, being encouraged by the gal-

* Lieutenant Thomas Chute succeeded to the vacancy caused by
the death of Captain Tew ; Ensign Richard Pennefather was
promoted Lieutenant ; and Serjeant-Major Thomas Stack was
appointed ensign in the TWENTY-SECOND regiment, the commissions
being dated 18th February, 1843, the day following the battle of
Meeanee.

lant example of their officers, displayed that heroism which 1843 adorns the British military character. Privates J. Doherty, C. Lynar, E. Jobin, J. McCartin, J. Walmsley, G. Roberts, E. Watson and J. Oakley, shot the defenders, and then captured fourteen standards, and made five prisoners. Privates S. Cowen, S. Alder, and G. Banbury also captured standards ; and Corporal Tim. Kelly shot one of the Scindians, and took from him a silver-knobbed standard. The Beloochee infantry and artillery fought well, but were unable, although greatly superior in numbers, to resist the determined attack of disciplined soldiers.

Major-General Sir Charles Napier stated in his public despatch. " The battle was decided by the troop of Horse " Artillery, and Her Majesty's TWENTY-SECOND regiment.

· " Of Lieutenant McMurdo's abilities as Acting As- " sistant Quartermaster-General, I cannot speak too " highly ; and regret to say, he has received a sabre " wound from a Beloochee, the third that he cut down in " single combat during the day.

" To the commanders of brigades and regiments, and " the officers, non-commissioned officers, and privates " under their command, I have to return my thanks for " their valiant bearing in the action."

The loss of the enemy was very great, and eleven pieces of cannon were taken in position on the nullah, together with seventeen standards. The Beloochee force was completely defeated, and their commander, Meer Shere Mahomed, fled to the desert.* Among the killed was

---

* The following interesting circumstance is recorded by Major-General Napier, in his history of the conquest of Scinde, respecting the march into the desert in pursuit of Meer Shere Mahomed :—

" On one of those long marches, which were almost continual, the " Twenty-fifth Sepoys, being nearly maddened by thirst and heat, " saw one of their water-carriers approaching with full skins of water ;

1843 the great promoter of the war, Hoche Mahomed Seedee.
Twenty-three rank and file of the regiment were killed
on this occasion; Lieutenants Thomas Chute, Henry J.
Coote, H. A. G. Evans, and John Brennan, Ensign
Richard Pennefather, six serjeants, one drummer, four
corporals, and one hundred and twenty-three privates
wounded. At the battle of Hyderabad, the regiment
mustered only five hundred and sixty-two rank and file;
the remainder being sick and convalescent, having been
left at Sukkur in Upper Scinde.

As a mark of Royal approbation for these victories,
Her Majesty, on the 4th of July, 1843, was pleased to ap-
point Major-General Sir Charles James Napier a Knight
Grand Cross of the Most Honorable Military Order of
the Bath; Lieutenant-Colonel Pennefather,* Brevet Lieu-

" they rushed towards him in crowds, tearing away the skins and
" struggling together, with loud cries of Water! Water! At that
" moment, some half-dozen straggling soldiers of the TWENTY-SECOND
" came up, apparently exhausted, and asked for some. At once the
" generous Indians withheld their hands from the skins, forgot their
" own sufferings, and gave the fainting Europeans to drink; then
" they all moved on, the Sepoys carrying the TWENTY-SECOND men's
" muskets for them, patting them on the shoulders, and encouraging
" them to hold out. It was in vain; they did so for a short time,
" but soon fell. It was then discovered that these noble fellows
" were all wounded, some deeply, but thinking there was to be
" another fight, they had concealed their hurts, and forced nature to
" sustain the loss of blood, the pain of wounds, the burning sun,
" the long marches, and the sandy desert, that their last moments
" might be given to their country on another field of battle!"

Names of men of the TWENTY-SECOND *regiment who concealed their
wounds, received in the Battle of Hyderabad, and marched with
their regiment the next day, thinking another battle was at hand.*

Serjeant Haney. John Durr, John Muldowney, Robert Young,
Henry Lines, Patrick Gill, James Andrews, Thomas Middleton,
James Mulvey, and Silvester Day.

* Lieutenant-Colonel Pennefather was appointed Aide-de-Camp
to the Queen, with the rank of Colonel, in 1846, the honor having
been deferred until this period in consequence of his short standing

tenant-Colonel Poole, Brevet Majors Frederick George, 1843
and Thomas Conway, were also nominated Companions
of the Bath, and their brevet rank was dated from the
above period.

Her Majesty was also graciously pleased to command
that a medal should be conferred upon the Officers, Non-
commissioned Officers, and Soldiers engaged in the battles.
of Meeanee and Hyderabad.

On the 18th of August, 1843, the TWENTY-SECOND
received the Royal authority to bear upon the regimental
or second colour, and on the appointments, the word
"SCINDE," in commemoration of its distinguished gallantry in the campaign against the Ameers of that
country, during the early part of the year 1843.

Her Majesty, on the 2nd of July, 1844, conferred
increased honor on the TWENTY-SECOND, by authorising
the corps to bear on the regimental colour and appointments, in addition to the word "SCINDE," the words
"MEEANEE" and "HYDERABAD," in commemoration of
the distinguished gallantry displayed in the general
engagements fought at those places respectively, on the
17th of February, and 24th of March, 1843.

On the 12th of February, 1844, the thanks of Parliament were voted to Major-General Sir Charles Napier,
G.C.B., and to the troops under his command, "*for the
"*eminent skill, energy, and gallantry, displayed by him in
"*the recent military operations in* SCINDE, *particularly in*

---

as a Lieutenant-Colonel in 1843, the year in which the victories of
Meeanee and Hyderabad were gained.

Colonel Pennefather exchanged to the Twenty-eighth Regiment,
with Lieut.-Colonel S. J. Cotton, on the 2nd December, 1847, and
becoming supernumerary on the arrival of the Twenty-eighth
regiment from India in 1848, was placed on half-pay. In August,
1848, Colonel Pennefather was appointed to serve on the Staff of
the army in Ireland.

1843 " *the two decisive battles of* MEEANEE *and* HYDERABAD ;"
to the several officers serving under Sir Charles Napier,
"*for their unwearied zeal and conspicuous gallantry ;*" and
to the troops, "*for their brave and meritorious conduct.*"

Major-General Sir Charles Napier, on presenting the
regiments at Kurrachee with the Medals conferred on them
for their gallantry in this campaign, addressed the soldiers
as follows :—

"Soldiers! the Battle of *Meeanee* is among those of
" which history will speak as proving the superiority of
" *discipline* over numbers ; and it is well, Soldiers! that we
" should dwell upon these things ; that we may understand
" how Medals are won, and why they are bestowed.

" Had we been without discipline, valour alone would
" not have won the victories of *Meeanee* and *Hyderabad!*
" Valour is like the *Strength* of a man, Discipline is like
" his *Mind,* that directs his strength to effective exertion.
" If two pugilists have a boxing-match, and one strikes
" at random, while the other boxes with science, planting
" every blow home, we know how the fight must be soon
" decided. So it is with two armies,—the one disciplined,
" the other without discipline, The General of the dis-
" ciplined Army directs his columns upon that part of the
" enemy's position which he deems to be the weakest ; as
" the mind of the boxer directs his blow against the opening
" offered by his unskilful enemy. But this is not all,—
" obedience to orders (which is discipline) enables us to
" bring up all the necessary provisions of war to the day
" and to the hour ; thus food and ammunition are at hand
" to support the blow of battle, just as the shoulder and
" the body are thrown forward to support and give vigour
" to the blow of the pugilist. But not only is valour
" useless without discipline, but it is even dangerous ;
" for without discipline the rashly brave would run

" heedlessly against the enemy, the cautious would seek 1843
" 'vantage ground, and the timid would retreat. Thus
" the Army would be scattered : but when an Army is
" disciplined, the ponderous charges of Cavalry, the steady
" tramp of the advancing Infantry, preparing to charge
" with a mighty shout, and the rolling thunder of Artillery
" pouring forth its iron shower, all combine simultaneously
" to strike and overthrow the enemy. Thus, Soldiers,
" are Medals won, more by discipline than by any ex-
" traordinary efforts of individual courage. To reward
" this obedience medals are bestowed, so that every man
" who wears this honoured badge is known to the world
" as one who, in the midst of the noise, the danger, and
" confusion of battle, had obeyed orders, and performed
" the three great duties of a Soldier—first, not to fire
" without orders ; next, when he does fire, to level low, so
" as to make sure of striking down an enemy ; thirdly, to
" keep his rank and dress upon his colours. The Medal
" tells the world that he has bravely done these things,
" and no man can walk with one of these Medals on his
" breast without feeling the conscious pride of an intrepid
" Soldier ! His caste may be high caste, or it may be
" low caste, but the Soldier, who bears on his breast a
" medal won in battle, is above all the castes in the world.
" The pleasure of giving you these Medals, Soldiers of
" the 12th Regiment (Native Infantry), is indeed great to
" me. I saw your valiant conduct, and I rejoice in distri-
" buting the reward which you honorably earned, and my
" satisfaction is increased by the presence of so large a
" body of Europeans, for it affords me an opportunity of
" saying to my countrymen that they will find these swarthy
" warriors of the East stanch and true in action as they
" were at Meeanee and Hyderabad, when they followed
" the example set them by the glorious TWENTY-SECOND

1843 " regiment. They will fight to the last drop of their blood,
" and stand or fall by the side of their European comrades.
" If the Almighty so wills it, that in these eventful times,
" War should again arise, and that I am once more per-
" mitted to lead an Army into the field, I should go into
" action with perfect confidence in the courage of the
" Native Troops. I speak of what I know of their gallantry,
" not from what I hear, but from what I have seen, and
" from my own knowledge, of their daring courage.

" Here I must address myself in a more direct manner
" to the Officers now before me, and in justice to them
" say, that their conduct, and the conduct of all the British
" Officers in these two battles, was very noble. For several
" hours the two lines were fighting close to each other,
" and as I cast my eye along the field, I everywhere saw
" the British Officers display their worthiness as Military
" leaders, and with unflinching intrepidity animating their
" Soldiers to battle!   To them, therefore, I will now first
" distribute these honorable decorations."

The Governor then dismounted, and advancing to the
line of officers of several regiments, and who had not
before received their medals, his Excellency presented
each with the Medal,—the bands playing " God save the
Queen."

On giving that which belonged to Lieutenant Marston,
of the 25th N. I., the General observed,—" But for you,
Marston, I probably should not have had this pleasure ;"
alluding to this Officer having intrepidly thrown himself
in front of his General when attacked by a Beloochee
Chief, whom the Lieutenant cut down ere he could reach
the General.

On the 18th of April the regiment left Hyderabad, and
proceeded to Kurrachee, where the right wing and head-
quarters embarked on the 27th of April, and sailed to

Bombay. Previously to the embarkation of the regiment 1843 for Bombay, the following order was issued by Major-General Sir Charles Napier, Governor of Scinde :—

"*27th April,* 1843.

"TWENTY-SECOND Regiment!

"You well know why I send you to Bombay, and "you also know how much I dislike doing so. But no-"thing shall stand in the way of your health and well-"being, that I have the power to remove. Cut up by "Disease and by Battle, you require rest, that you may "again join us, and add to the Laurels with which you are "already decorated.

"C. J. NAPIER, *Major-General,*
                    Governor."

The reception of the regiment at Bombay, on the 2nd of May, was distinguished by high marks of honor, by command of the Governor, on which occasion the accompanying order was issued :—

"*Bombay, Monday, 1st May,* 1843.

"GARRISON ORDERS.

"By the Honorable the Governor.—The Head-"Quarters of Her Majesty's TWENTY-SECOND Regi-"ment of Foot having arrived from Scinde, will be dis-"embarked to-morrow morning at sunrise.

"On this occasion the Governor and Commander-in-"Chief of the Garrison, desirous of paying every mark of "honor to this distinguished Corps, will himself receive "it at the Apollo Pier.

"On the landing of the first Division, a Royal Salute "is to be fired from the Saluting Battery.

"The Troops composing the Garrison will be drawn "up in Review Order, in a convenient position, and will "salute Her Majesty's TWENTY-SECOND regiment, as it "passes on its way to Fort George Barracks.

1843   " His Excellency directs the attendance of all Military
" Officers at the Presidency who may not be sick, or
" engaged on other duty.
" The Commandant of the Garrison is requested to
" carry out the above order.

"BRUCE SETON, *Major,*
Town Major."

The General Staff of the Garrison testified their admiration of the gallant conduct of the regiment, by giving a
public banquet to the Officers of the corps ; and the
inhabitants of Bombay, including the Civil Authorities,
raised a handsome subscription, to be applied to the
benefit of the sufferers in the regiment, widows and
orphans, by the Campaign in Scinde.

The left wing landed at Panwell on the 16th of May,
and proceeded from thence to Poonah, where it arrived on
the 23rd of May.   The right wing and head-quarters
arrived at Poonah, from Bombay, on the 1st of June.

General the Honorable Edward Finch died on the 27th
of October, 1843, and the colonelcy of the regiment was conferred on Major-General Sir Charles James Napier, K.C.B.

1844   On the 17th and 18th of October, 1844, the regiment
marched from Poonah in wings to Bowree, and on the
19th the whole moved together for Field Service in the
Kolápore districts, where the regiment lost two officers,
and thirty non-commissioned officers and privates, by
cholera.

A portion of the regiment was employed in taking the
north pettah under the walls of the fort of Punalla, on the
27th of November ; on the 28th, 29th, and 30th of
November the regiment, under the command of Brevet
Lieut.-Colonel John Poole, was employed in the investment
of *Punalla* and *Pownghur,* and on the 1st of December
was at the capture of those forts, the latter of which was

taken by the regiment. During these operations the 1844
TWENTY-SECOND formed part of the third brigade of the
force employed under Major-General Delamotte.

On the 26th of December a wing of the regiment
marched, and joined the first brigade on service in the
Sawunt-Warree district ; the other wing remained near
Kolapore.

On the 31st of December, 1844, a wing of the regiment
arrived at Susseedroog from Kolapore, and joined the
first brigade of the Field Force in the Sawunt-Warree
country, and was employed in investing the forts of
Monuhurr and Monsentosh, and participated in all the
operations for driving the enemy out of their stockades
in the densely wooded country between Susseedroog and
the Forts.

The regiment had several skirmishes with the enemy ;
on the 17th of January, 1845, part of the wing descended 1845
the Elephant rock with other troops, and took the village
of Seevapore, in the Concan, close under Fort Monuhurr,
where one man was killed and seven wounded. The whole
of the soldiers were employed, part in the Deccan or
heights above, and part in the Concan close under the
forts, investing them from the 17th to the 26th of January,
during which period the forts were constantly shelled by
the British artillery, the enemy from the forts firing their
great guns and musketry.

On the night of the 26th of January the enemy vacated
the forts unperceived, and escaped through a dense jungle,
leaving the forts in the possession of the Anglo-Indian army.

The wing joined the regiment at Kolapore on the 6th
of February, escorting prisoners taken during the insurrection. The regiment was employed in doing duty
over about six hundred prisoners until its recal to Poonah,
for which place it marched on the 16th of April, and
arrived on the 2nd of May, 1845.

1845 A wing of the regiment, consisting of four hundred rank and file, under the command of Captain Souter, marched from Poonah for Bombay on the 25th of December, 1845.

1846 The head-quarters of the regiment, under the command of Lieutenant Colonel Samuel Brandram Boileau, consisting of five companies, marched from Poonah to Bombay on the 15th of August, 1846, and joined the wing of the TWENTY-SECOND at that station. The march was performed in the middle of the monsoon, in eight days, rain consequently falling nearly the whole of the way.

The regiment remained together at Bombay, having six companies at Colaba, and three at Fort George, until the 14th of November, 1846, when the head-quarters, with five of the companies which were stationed at Colaba, were ordered to Poonah, in consequence of fever of a malarious nature having attacked the men, nearly every soldier at Colaba having been admitted into hospital in less than two months; the casualties were very numerous.

1847 The left wing, consisting of four companies, marched from Bombay on the 12th of January, 1847, and arrived at Poonah on the 21st of January. During the year

1848 1848 the regiment continued to be stationed at Poonah.

1849 On the 25th of January, 1849, the regiment proceeded to Bombay, and was subsequently stationed at Colaba. The left wing, consisting of four companies, embarked for Kurrachee on the 24th of January.

In June, 1849, the period to which the Record has been extended, the regiment remained at Colaba, and consisted of fifty-three serjeants, nineteen drummers, and 1042 rank and file, under the command of Lieutenant-Colonel Sydney John Cotton, Lieutenant-Colonel Boileau being in command of the Poonah brigade.

1849.

Description of the Beloochee Standard captured at the Battle of MEEANEE, *on the 17th of February,* 1843.

THE Beloochee Standard, represented in the engraving, was taken at the Battle of *Meeanee*, on the 17th of February, 1843, by Private James O'Neill of the TWENTY-SECOND regiment, as narrated at page 35 of the Historical Record. The Standard is triangular; the longest side is about seven feet in length, and the other sides measure each about five feet. The Staff is nine feet in length.

The Standards captured at the Battle of *Hyderabad*, on the 24th of March, 1843, were of a similar rude description, and do not afford a just idea of the Army which they may be supposed to have led on. No person, on viewing these Trophies, would suppose the Beloochee Army, to which they belonged, to have been composed of men so gallant and so formidable; so well armed, and so expert in the use of their arms, as the Scindian troops proved themselves in these battles.

Description of the Silver Medal struck in commemoration of the Victories of MEEANEE *and* HYDERABAD, *and conferred on the Officers and Men engaged in those Battles.*

ON the obverse; the bust of HER MAJESTY, with the inscription " VICTORIA REGINA."

On the reverse; the words " MEEANEE," " HYDERABAD," " 1843," enclosed within branches of Laurel, and surmounted by the Imperial Crown.

SUCCESSION OF COLONELS

OF

THE TWENTY-SECOND,

OR

THE CHESHIRE REGIMENT OF FOOT.

HENRY, DUKE OF NORFOLK, K.G.

Appointed 16th March, 1689.

LORD HENRY HOWARD, son of Henry, Earl of Norwich, afterwards Duke of Norfolk, was summoned to parliament in 1678, by the title of Lord Mowbray: and on the death of Prince Rupert, in 1682, his lordship was nominated governor and constable of Windsor Castle, and warden of the forest of Windsor; also lord lieutenant of Berkshire and Surrey. On the decease of his father, in 1684, he succeeded to the dignity of DUKE OF NORFOLK, and of Earl Marshal of England; and in May, 1685, he was elected a Knight of the most noble order of the Garter. On the breaking out of the rebellion of the DUKE OF MONMOUTH, the DUKE OF NORFOLK took great interest in raising a regiment of foot for the service of King James II., now the twelfth regiment of foot, of which he was appointed colonel. His Grace did not approve of the measures of the court, and evinced a strong attachment to the protestant religion. One day (says Bishop Burnet) the King gave the DUKE OF NORFOLK the sword of state to carry with him to the Popish chapel, which he carried as far as the door and then stopped, not being willing to enter the chapel. The King said, " My Lord, your father would have

" gone farther;" to which the Duke answered,—" Your
" Majesty's father was the better man, and he would not
" have gone so far." His Grace resigned his regiment, and
joined in the invitation to the PRINCE OF ORANGE. When
the Prince landed, the DUKE OF NORFOLK was in London,
and was one of the Peers who petitioned the King for a free
parliament. He afterwards proceeded to his seat in Norfolk,
declared for the Prince of Orange, and brought that and
some of the neighbouring counties into the Prince's interest.
On the elevation of the Prince of Orange to the throne, his
Grace was sworn a member of the privy council ; and afterwards used his interest and influence in raising a corps of infantry, now the TWENTY SECOND REGIMENT, of which he
was appointed colonel in March, 1689 ; but he resigned his
commission in the same year. He died on the 2nd of April
1701.

SIR HENRY BELLASIS, KT.

Appointed 28th September, 1689.

SIR HENRY BELLASIS was educated in strict principles of
loyalty and attachment to monarchical government, and when
a youth he suffered in the royal cause during the usurpation
of Cromwell. Soon after the restoration he was nominated
captain of an independent company in garrison at Hull, of
which fortress the Lord Bellasis (or Belasyse) was appointed
governor ; but he resigned, in 1673, in consequence of the
Test Act, he being a Roman Catholic. In the summer of
1674, Sir Henry Bellasis raised a company of musketeers and
pikemen for the service of the United Provinces of the Netherlands, and was engaged at the siege of Grave in the
autumn of that year. He also served at the siege of Maestricht
in 1676 ; at the battle of Mont-Cassel in 1677 ; and in the
following spring he succeeded Colonel Ashley in the command of a regiment which is now the sixth foot. At the
battle of St. Denis, in 1678, he evinced signal valour and
ability, vying in feats of gallantry with his commanders the
Prince of Orange and the celebrated Earl of Ossory, and was
wounded. During the rebellion of the Duke of Monmouth,

E

in 1685, he accompanied his regiment to England; and in 1687 circumstances occurred which occasioned him to withdraw from the Dutch service; but he preserved his attachment to the Protestant interest and to the Prince of Orange. In 1689 he succeeded the Duke of Norfolk in the colonelcy of the TWENTY-SECOND regiment, with which corps he served in Ireland under the veteran Duke Schomberg. He served as brigadier-general under King William in 1690; was at the battle of the Boyne; and at the siege of Limerick, where he again distinguished himself. In 1691 he acquired new honours at the siege of Athlone; he also displayed bravery and judgment at the battle of Aghrim; and on the reduction of Galway he was appointed governor of that fortress, and took possession of the town on the 26th of July, with his own and two other regiments of foot. The rank of major-general was conferred on this distinguished officer in April, 1692, and he commanded a brigade under King William in Flanders, in the autumn of that year. He acquired additional reputation at the battle of Landen, in 1693; also in the command of a brigade under King William during the following campaign; and in October, 1694, his Majesty rewarded him with the rank of lieut.-general. His meritorious conduct procured him the favour and confidence of his Sovereign, by whom he was employed on important services. He commanded the camp on the Bruges canal, in May, 1695; and a division of the covering army was placed under his orders during the siege of Namur. At the close of the campaign he was appointed president of the general court-martial which tried the officers who surrendered Dixmude and Deinse to the enemy, and sentenced Major-General Ellemberg to be shot. He continued to serve in the Netherlands until the peace of Ryswick. In 1701 he obtained the colonelcy of the Queen Dowager's regiment (now second foot) in exchange with Colonel Selwyn. In 1702 he was second in command of the British troops in the expedition to Cadiz; and having been charged with participating in the plunder of Port St. Mary, he was tried by a court-martial and dismissed the service. His reputation was thus unfortunately tarnished; but his crime does not appear to have been considered of a heinous nature, as he was subsequently elected a member of parliament for the city of Durham; was appointed by Queen Anne, in

1711, one of the commissioners to inquire into several particulars respecting the accounts of the army in Spain ; and in June, 1713, he was appointed governor of Berwick. He died on the 14th of December, 1717.

WILLIAM SELWYN.

Appointed 28th June, 1701.

WILLIAM SELWYN served in the army of the United Provinces of the Netherlands, in the time of King Charles II., and afterwards held a commission under the British crown. In 1688 he was nominated captain and lieut.-colonel in the second foot guards, with which corps he served in Flanders, and in 1691 King William gave him the colonelcy of the second foot, vacant by the decease of Lieut.-General Kirke. He served at the head of his regiment at the battle of Landen on the 29th of July, 1693, and distinguished himself under the eye of his sovereign ; he also served at the siege of Namur, in the summer of 1695, and was promoted to the rank of brigadier-general during the siege. He subsequently commanded a brigade of infantry in the Netherlands, under King William III., who nominated him governor of the island of Jamaica. He exchanged to the TWENTY-SECOND regiment in 1701 ; and was promoted to the rank of major-general on the 10th June, 1702. He died in June, 1702.

THOMAS HANDASYD.

Appointed 20th June, 1702.

AFTER a progressive service in the subordinate commissions, THOMAS HANDASYD was promoted to the lieut.-colonelcy of the TWENTY-SECOND regiment, with which corps he proceeded to the island of Jamaica; and in June, 1702, Queen Anne promoted him to the colonelcy of the regiment. He served in the West Indies ; was advanced to the rank of brigadier-general in 1705, and to that of major-general in 1710. In

1712, he resigned the colonelcy of the TWENTY-SECOND regiment in favour of his son.

ROGER HANDASYD.

Appointed 3rd April, 1712.

THIS Officer served many years in the TWENTY-SECOND regiment, and was promoted by Queen Anne to that lieut.-colonelcy of that corps, which he commanded some time at the island of Jamaica. He succeeded his father in the colonelcy of the regiment in 1712 ; was removed to the sixteenth foot in 1730,—promoted to the rank of brigadier-general in 1735,—to that of major-general in 1739,—and to lieut.-general in 1743. He died in 1763.

WILLIAM BARRELL.

Appointed 25th August, 1730.

THIS officer entered the army in the reign of William III. ; he obtained the rank of captain in 1698, and his distinguished conduct in the wars of Queen Anne was rewarded with the brevet rank of colonel on the 1st of January, 1707. In 1715 he was promoted to the colonelcy of the twenty-eighth foot ; in 1727 he was appointed brigadier-general ; in 1730 he was removed to the TWENTY-SECOND regiment, and in 1734 to the King's Own. In the following year he was promoted to the rank of major-general ; in 1739 to that of lieut.-general ; and he was also appointed governor of Pendennis Castle. He died on the 9th of August, 1749.

THE HONORABLE JAMES ST. CLAIR.

Appointed 30th October, 1734.

THE HONORABLE JAMES ST. CLAIR entered the army in the reign of Queen Anne, and served under the celebrated JOHN DUKE OF MARLBOROUGH. He was several years an officer in the third foot guards, in which corps he rose to the commission of major, with the rank of colonel, and in 1734 King George II. nominated him to the colonelcy of the TWENTY-SECOND regiment, from which he was removed, in 1737, to the first, the royal regiment. In 1739 he was promoted to the rank of brigadier-general; in 1741 to that of major-general; and to that of lieut.-general in 1745, at which time he was performing the duty of quarter master-general in the Netherlands, to the army commanded by His Royal Highness the Duke of Cumberland. In the following year he commanded an expedition which was originally designed for the attack of the French settlements in Canada; but was countermanded, and afterwards proceeded against the French seaport L'Orient and the peninsula of Quiberon; no important results were, however, achieved. He was subsequently employed on an embassy to the courts of Vienna and Turin.* On the decease of his brother, in 1750, he became entitled to the dignity of Lord Sinclair, a Scottish peerage; but he preferred a seat in the House of Commons, of which he had been many years a member, and therefore did not assume the title. In 1761 he was promoted to the rank of general. He died at Dysart, in November, 1762.

JOHN MOYLE.

Appointed 27th June, 1737

JOHN MOYLE entered the army in the reign of Queen Anne, and served with reputation under the celebrated John Duke of Marlborough; he rose to the lieut.-colonelcy of a newly raised regiment of foot, and in 1708 was promoted to the rank of colonel in the army. At the peace of Utrecht his regiment was disbanded. In 1723 King George I. conferred the colonelcy of the thirty-sixth regiment on Colonel Moyle, who was promoted to the rank of brigadier-general in 1727, and to that of major-general in 1735: in 1737 he was removed to the TWENTY-SECOND regiment. He died on the 3rd of November, 1738.

---

* David Hume, the historian, was secretary to General St. Clair, during the expedition to the coast of France, and the embassy to Vienna and Turin.

THOMAS PAGET.

Appointed 13th December, 1738.

THIS officer entered the army in the reign of King William III., and was many years an officer of the eighth horse, now seventh dragoon guards, with which corps he served under the celebrated John Duke of Marlborough. On the 1st of August, 1710, he was promoted to the lieut.-colonelcy of the eighth horse : he was afterwards lieut.-colonel of the first troop of horse grenadier guards; and in July, 1732, was nominated colonel of the thirty-second regiment, from which he was removed, in 1738, to the TWENTY-SECOND. In 1739 he was promoted to the rank of brigadier-general. He died on the 28th of May, 1741.

RICHARD O'FARRELL.

Appointed 12th August, 1741.

RICHARD O'FARRELL was nominated ensign in a regiment of foot on the 1st of May, 1692; and he served with reputation in the wars of King William III. and of Queen Anne. On the 20th of December, 1722, he was promoted to the lieut.-colonelcy of the ninth foot, and he performed the duties of commanding officer to that corps many years, with credit to himself and advantage to the service. On the decease of Brigadier-General Paget, in 1741, King George II. rewarded the long and faithful services of Lieut.-Colonel O'Farrell with the colonelcy of the TWENTY-SECOND regiment. In 1746 Colonel O'Farrell was promoted to the rank of brigadier-general, and in 1754 to that of major-general. His decease occurred in 1757.

EDWARD WHITMORE.

Appointed 11th July, 1757.

EDWARD WHITMORE entered the army in the reign of King George II., and serving with distinction in the wars of the

Austrian succession, was promoted to the lieut.-colonelcy of the thirty-sixth regiment on the 17th of July, 1747. He performed the duty of commanding officer of the thirty-sixth regiment with reputation ten years; and in July, 1757, King George II. rewarded him with the colonelcy of the TWENTY-SECOND regiment. He was nominated brigadier-general in America in December, 1757; in 1758 he commanded a brigade under Lieut.-General (afterwards Lord) Amherst, in the descent on Cape Breton, and at the siege and capture of Louisburg, of which fortress he was afterwards nominated governor. On the 19th of February, 1761, he was promoted to the rank of major-general. During the following winter he left Louisburg for Boston; during the voyage the ship was driven, by severe weather, into the harbour of Plymouth, and Major-General Whitmore, being on deck, in the night, fell overboard and was drowned.

THE HONORABLE THOMAS GAGE.

Appointed 29th March, 1762.

THE HONORABLE THOMAS GAGE, second son of Thomas, first Viscount Gage, of Castle Island, in Ireland, having served some time in the subordinate commissions, was appointed major of the forty-fourth foot in February, 1747; and he was further promoted to the lieut.-colonelcy of the regiment on the 2nd of March, 1751. He was serving with his regiment in America, when a dispute occurred between Great Britain and France respecting the territory on the banks of the Ohio, and he commanded the advance-guard of the forces sent against Fort Du Quesne, which the French had built to command the entrance into the country on the Ohio and Mississippi. In the disastrous action on the 9th of July, 1755, Major-General Braddock was killed, and Lieut.-Colonel the Honorable Thomas Gage was wounded. He continued to serve in America, where he raised a provincial regiment, which was numbered the eightieth, light-armed foot, of which he was appointed colonel in May, 1758; he was also appointed brigadier general in North America, and the efforts of the army effected the conquest of Canada, which has continued to form part of the British dominions from that period. He was promoted to the rank of major-general in 1761, and in the same year he performed the duty of Commander-in-Chief in North America, and also succeeded Sir Jeffrey Amherst as Colonel-in-Chief of the sixtieth regiment, which he held two months, when Lieut.-General Amherst was·re-appointed. In March, 1762, he was appointed colonel of the TWENTY-SECOND foot; and in April, 1770, he was promoted to the rank of lieut.-general. When the misunderstanding between Great Britain and her North American colonies began to assume a serious aspect, he was appointed Captain-General and Governor-in-Chief of Massachusetts Bay, and he arrived at Boston in May, 1774. Hostilities commenced in the following year, and his active exertions to suppress the rebellion were rewarded in August, 1775, with the appointment of Commander-in-Chief in North America, which he resigned in a few months afterwards. In April, 1782, he was appointed colonel of the seventeenth light dragoons; he was promoted to the rank of general in November following, and in 1785 he was removed to the eleventh dragoons. He died in 1787.

CHARLES O'HARA.

Appointed 18th April, 1782.

CHARLES O'HARA was appointed cornet in the third dragoons in December, 1752, and in 1756 he was promoted to lieutenant and captain in the second foot guards. He served in Portugal in 1762, and performed the duties of quartermaster-general to the army under Lieut.-General the Earl of Loudoun. In 1769 he was promoted to the rank of captain and lieut.-colonel; and he served with his regiment in North America. In the autumn of 1781 he was promoted to the rank of major-general. He commanded the brigade of foot guards under Lieut.-General Earl Cornwallis, in Virginia; distinguished himself at the passage of the Catawba river on the 1st of February, 1781; and was wounded at the battle of Guildford on the 15th of March. In 1782 he was nominated to the colonelcy of the TWENTY-SECOND regiment; was removed to the seventy-fourth highlanders in 1791, and was advanced to the rank of lieut.-general in 1793. He commanded the British troops at Toulon, and was wounded and taken prisoner in an action with the French republican troops on the 30th of November, 1793. His services were rewarded with the appointment of governor of Gibraltar, and in 1798 he was promoted to the rank of general. It is recorded that he possessed a happy combination of talents ; was a brave and enterprising soldier, a strict disciplinarian, and a polite and accomplished gentleman. He died at Gibraltar on the 21st of February, 1802.

DAVID DUNDAS.

Appointed 2nd April, 1791.

DAVID DUNDAS was one of the most distinguished officers of the age in which he lived, for his perfect knowledge of the principles of military tactics. He commenced his military education at the age of thirteen in the academy at Woolwich, and at fifteen he assisted in a survey of Scotland ; in 1756 he obtained a commission in the fifty-sixth regiment. In 1758 he proceeded with the expedition to the coast of France as an assistant quartermaster-general ; and in the following year obtained the command of a troop in a newly raised regiment of light dragoons (Eliott's light horse), now the fifteenth, or King's hussars. He served with his regiment in Germany in 1760 and 1761 ; in the following summer he accompanied an expedition to Cuba, as aide-de-camp to Major-General Eliott, and was actively employed in the reduction of the Havannah.   After the peace he resumed his post in his regiment, in which he rose to the rank of major ; and, urged by an ardent desire to acquire a perfect knowledge of every branch of his profession, he obtained permission to proceed to the Continent, to observe the practice of the French and Austrian armies.   In 1775 he obtained the lieut.-colonelcy of the twelfth light dragoons, joined the regiment in Ireland shortly afterwards, and in 1778 received the appointment of quartermaster-general in that country.   In 1782 he was removed to the lieut.-colonelcy of the second Irish horse, now the fifth dragoon guards.   In 1785 he again proceeded to the Continent, attended the exercises of the Prussian troops during

three summers, and after his return he presented His Majesty
with a detailed account of their evolutions.

Colonel Dundas, having become a proficient tactician, produced, in 1788, a highly useful work on the principles of military
movements, which became the basis of our army regula-
tions for field exercises and movements. His abilities obtained
for him the favour and attention of King George III., who
appointed him adjutant-general in Ireland, for the purpose of
introducing his system of tactics into the army of that country.
In 1790 Colonel Dundas was promoted to the rank of major-
general. In 1791 he obtained the colonelcy of the TWENTY-
SECOND foot, and in the same year was placed on the Irish
staff, but he resigned that appointment in 1793 to engage in
service of actual warfare. After the commencement of
hostilities with the French republic, Major-General Dundas
was employed on a military mission to the island of Jersey,
and was subsequently sent to the Continent to confer with the
Duke of York respecting the siege of Dunkirk. From
Flanders he proceeded to Toulon, where he commanded under
Lieut.-General O'Hara, and when the lieut.-general was
taken prisoner, he succeeded to the command of the garrison.
His services there, although he was ultimately obliged to
evacuate the place, called forth the approbation of his Sovereign
and of the British nation. After abandoning Toulon, he
made a descent on Corsica, which island was reduced and
annexed to the British dominions; but shortly afterwards he
received directions to proceed to Flanders, where he arrived
in the spring of 1794, and commanded a brigade of cavalry at
the battle of Tournay on the 22nd of May, 1794. Major-
General Dundas was actively employed in the retreat through
Holland, and the corps under his immediate command gained
considerable advantage over the enemy in two successive
actions near Gelder-Malsen; he highly distinguished himself
also in an attack upon the French post at Thuyl, in December
of the same year. He continued with the British troops in
Germany during the summer of 1795, and in December was
appointed colonel of the seventh light dragoons. After
his return to England he was appointed quartermaster-
general to the army; and he composed the celebrated regula-
tions for the field exercises and movements for the cavalry,
which were approved by his Royal Highness the Duke of

York, and by King George III., and ordered to be exclusively adopted throughout the cavalry.

In 1799 Lieut.-General Dundas commanded a division of the allied army under the Duke of York, in the expedition to Holland; he distinguished himself in several actions with the enemy, and was highly commended by His Royal Highness in his public despatches. In 1801 he was appointed colonel of the second, or Royal North British dragoons, and was constituted governor of Fort George. In 1802 he was promoted to the rank of general; and in the following year, when the French were preparing to invade England, he was placed in command of the troops in the southern district, which comprised the counties of Kent and Sussex. In 1804 he was appointed governor of the Royal Hospital at Chelsea, and created a Knight of the Bath. On the 18th of March, 1809, His Majesty was pleased to confer on this distinguished veteran the appointment of Commander-in-chief of the army, on the resignation of Field-Marshal His Royal Highness the Duke of York, which appointment he held until the 25th of May, 1811, when His Royal Highness was re-appointed. He was also appointed colonel-in-chief of the rifle brigade on the 31st of August, 1809. He was promoted to the colonelcy of the King's dragoon guards on the 27th of Januuary, 1813. He died in 1820, after a distinguished service of upwards of sixty years.

WILLIAM CROSBIE.

Appointed 23rd December, 1795.

AFTER serving in the subordinate commissions, WILLIAM CROSBIE was nominated captain of a company in the twenty-eighth regiment, on the 9th of May, 1769; and in October, 1778, he was promoted to the majority of the seventh Royal Fusiliers, with which corps he served in the Carolinas; in April, 1781, he obtained the lieut.-colonelcy of the TWENTY-SECOND regiment. While stationed at Windsor in 1785, he obtained the permission of King George III. for the introduction of an order of merit in the corps, which under his command obtained a high reputation for correct discipline.

He was promoted to the rank of colonel in 1790; and in 1793 received a letter of service for raising the eighty-ninth regiment, of which he was appointed colonel. In 1794 he was advanced to the rank of major-general, and was removed to the TWENTY-SECOND regiment in 1795. He died on the 16th of June, 1798, at Portsmouth, of which fortress he was lieut.-governor at the time of his decease.

JOHN GRAVES SIMCOE.

Appointed 18*th June*, 1798.

JOHN GRAVES SIMCOE, son of Captain Simcoe of the Royal Navy, evinced great talent from his youth. It is recorded that, when a boy, he was taken prisoner at sea, and conveyed up the river St. Lawrence, to Quebec; and he constructed a chart of the river, which was given to Major-General Wolfe, who sailed with an expedition against Quebec, in 1759. On the 27th of April, 1770, he was appointed ensign in the thirty-fifth regiment, with which corps he served at Boston, in 1775; he was appointed captain in the fortieth regiment in December, 1775, and served at Long Island and New York in 1776, and in the expedition to Pennsylvania in 1777, when he distinguished himself at the battle of Brandywine, and was wounded. In October of the same year, he was placed at the head of a provincial corps, called " The Queen's Rangers," with the rank of major-commandant, and was promoted to the rank of lieut.-colonel in 1778. His services with this corps are spoken of by Lieut.-General Sir Henry Clinton, in a letter to Lord George Germaine, in the following terms :—" Lieut.-Colonel Simcoe has been at the head of a " battalion since October, 1777, and since that time he has " been perpetually with the advance of the army. The his- " tory of the corps under his command is a series of gallant, " skilful, and successful enterprises against the enemy, without " a single reverse. The Queen's Rangers have killed, or .`" taken, twice their own numbers. Colonel Simcoe himself " has been thrice wounded; and I do not scruple to assert, " that his successes have been no less the fruit of the most ex- " tensive knowledge of his profession which study and the

" experience within his reach could give him, than of the
" most watchful attention and shining courage." After repeatedly distinguishing himself in North and South Carolina,
and Virginia, he was included in the capitulation of York
Town, and returned to England in a state of debility from
excessive exertion, &c. In 1790 he was promoted to the
rank of colonel, and in the following year raised a corps of
infantry called the Queen's Rangers, of which he was appointed colonel on the 1st of September, 1791. He subsequently proceeded to the West Indies, where he evinced the
same talent, energy, and courage which shone so conspicuously
in the American war. In 1794 he was promoted to the rank
of major-general, and in 1796 to the local rank of lieut.-
general in the island of St. Domingo. In January, 1798, he
was appointed Colonel of the eighty-first regiment, and was
removed, in June following, to the TWENTY-SECOND regiment,
the colonelcy of which corps he retained until his decease in
1806.

SIR JAMES H. CRAIG, K.B.

Appointed 30th October, 1806.

JAMES HENRY CRAIG was appointed ensign in the thirtieth
foot, in 1763, and served with his regiment at Gibraltar : in
1771 he was promoted to captain in the forty-seventh regiment, with which corps he served several campaigns in
America ; and in 1777 he was promoted to the majority, and
in 1781 to the lieut.-colonelcy, of the eighty-second regiment,
from which he was removed, in 1783, to the sixteenth. He
was promoted to the rank of colonel in 1790, and to that of
major-general in 1794 ; in 1795 he was nominated to the
colonelcy of the forty-sixth regiment : he was advanced to
the rank of lieut.-general in 1801, and removed to the eighty-
sixth in 1804. He commanded an expedition to the Medi-
terranean, in 1805, with the local rank of general, and the
dignity of a knight of the Bath ; the troops under his orders
landed at Naples, and subsequently took possession of the
island of Sicily. In 1806 he was removed to the TWENTY-
SECOND regiment ; and in 1807 he was appointed governor
of Upper and Lower Canada, with the local rank of general

in America; in 1809 he was removed to the seventy-eighth Highlanders. He was also appointed governor of Blackness Castle. He died on the 12th of January, 1812.

THE HONORABLE EDWARD FINCH.

Appointed 18*th September*, 1809.

IN 1778 the HONORABLE EDWARD FINCH was appointed cornet in the eleventh light dragoons, and in 1779 he was promoted to a lieutenancy in the eighty-seventh foot. He embarked for the West Indies, in January, 1780, and served there, and in North America, until 1782, when he returned to England, and was appointed lieutenant and captain in the second foot guards; in 1792 he was promoted to captain and lieut.-colonel in the same corps. He served the campaigns of 1793 and 1794, in Flanders, under His Royal Highness the Duke of York, and shared in the several actions in which the foot guards distinguished themselves. In 1796 he was promoted to the rank of colonel, and in 1799 he commanded the first battalion of his regiment in the expedition to Holland, where he served in several actions under Lieut.-General Sir Ralph Abercromby and His Royal Highness the Duke of York. He commanded the brigade of light cavalry in the expedition to Egypt, in 1800, with the rank of brigadier-general, and was promoted to the rank of major-general, in January, 1801. After commanding the light cavalry in Egypt some time, he was placed at the head of a brigade of infantry, and was honored with the Order of the Crescent from the Grand Seignior. He commanded a brigade of foot guards in the expedition to Hanover in 1805; and in 1807 he commanded a brigade at the capture of Copenhagen. In 1808 he was promoted to the rank of lieut.-general, and appointed colonel of the fifty-fourth regiment, and in 1809 he was removed to the TWENTY-SECOND. He was promoted to the rank of general in 1819. His decease occurred on the 27th of October, 1843.

Sir Charles James Napier, G.C.B.

Appointed 21st November, 1843.

The following Regimental Order was issued by Major-General Sir Charles Napier, upon his appointment by Her Majesty to the Colonelcy of the TWENTY-SECOND Regiment.

"TWENTY-SECOND!

" Her Majesty has been graciously pleased to place me "at your head, and I shall end my military career wearing the "uniform of the Regiment. Your Glory must be my Glory, "and well I know it will increase, when you have again an op-"portunity to use your Arms! Never were the Musket and "Bayonet wielded by stronger men, nor were the Royal Co-"lours of England ever confided to more intrepid Soldiers!

" Many General Officers have been made Colonels of Regi-"ments that they had formerly commanded, and with whose "glory their own fame is associated; but old Comrades have "passed away,—to the new men, they are strangers,—and "nought remains to bind them to their Regiments, but Me-"mory and Renown! My good fortune has been greater, for "while I rejoice in the past and present honors of my old "Corps, the Fiftieth Regiment, I am, as Colonel of the "TWENTY-SECOND, placed among men at whose head I have "so lately fought, and to whose valour I owe so much!!

" Soldiers, we are not men without feeling as *pseudo* Philoso-"phers pretend! Obedience, Discipline, War, they deprive "us not of Manly sentiments. I shall always have the strongest "attachment to the corps with whom I have served, and among "the honors won for me by the Army of Scinde, the greatest "is that of being your Colonel!!

(Signed)   " C. J. Napier, *Major-General,*
              " *Colonel 22nd Regiment.*

" *Kurrachee, 23rd January,* 1844."

The following Postscript to the Official letter to Major-General Sir Charles Napier, announcing his appointment as

Colonel of the TWENTY-SECOND Regiment, was in the *Duke of Wellington's own hand-writing* :—

"P. S. I recommended this arrangement to Her Majesty,
"principally on the ground that it would be satisfactory to you,
"as this was the only one of Her Majesty's Regiments in India
"engaged in the two glorious battles fought at *Meeanee* and
"*Hyderàbad,* in *Scinde;* and Her Majesty was graciously
"pleased to approve of the recommendation on that ground."

LONDON:

Printed by WILLIAM CLOWES and SONS, Stamford Street,
For Her Majesty's Stationery Office.

CPSIA information can be obtained at www.ICGtesting.com
Printed in the USA
LVOW102027120712

289841LV00010B/3/P